What the Enemy Has Stolen
God Has Promised to You
Now Is the Time to...

TAKE IT BACK!

by

Van Crouch

ALBURY PUBLISHING
Tulsa, Oklahoma

What the Enemy Has Stolen God Has Promised to You
Now Is the Time to... Take It Back!
ISBN 1-57778-021-3
Copyright © 1998 by
William V. Crouch
P. O. Box 320
Wheaton, Illinois 60187

Published by ALBURY PUBLISHING
P. O. Box 470406
Tulsa, Oklahoma 74147-0406

DEDICATION

To Doni and the "Take It Back" Team: Glen and Melaney, Robb and Wendy, Mark and Debra, and Brent.

Thanks for ten challenging but exciting years. Your vision for restoration has impacted me in a life-changing way and I love you all.

CONTENTS

Contents

INTRODUCTION

Did your twin brother or sister forget your birthday? Are you dragging through life like a piano player in a marching band? Or do you feel like you're wearing milk bone underwear in a dog-eat-dog world? Rather depressing, isn't it?

Does fear plague your life? Have creative ideas and new ventures slipped through your fingers because you have become paralyzed by fear? Has losing at life and adversity caused deep inner anger to the point where you are ready to give up?

Wait a minute! Read just a few paragraphs further, because there is good news for you. I know those feelings because I've been there too. At some point in life, we all face an hour of decision to give up or get back up in order to go up.

You may have faced a major loss in your life; however, you can *Take It Back!* It might be the loss of a loved one, the breakup of a marriage, the loss of a job, a financial loss, or a serious illness. You need to know your problem has a limited life span. Your failure is not fatal. Your defeat is not final. You can rise up in the presence of God's unchanging power and take back the ground you've lost.

I'm not suggesting it will be easy. The road to the next level in life is always uphill. But this book will show you how God took me from resounding failure to His promise of a purpose-filled future. These twelve chapters give the proactive plan of proven principles to attack your lack in any area of life which I learned in my own personal journey.

You see, since the beginning of time there has been a thief roaming planet earth. He comes to steal, kill, and destroy. This book provides a battle plan to put your adversary in the phone booth dialing 9-1-1, chugging antacid, and begging for mercy!

The main thing you need to know right now is: You can do it! God has been waiting for you to make a move. Someone said, "Ideas are a dime a dozen, but the people who use them are priceless." God has no shortage of ideas, but He desires to use those ideas to help you on the road to victory.

This is your day! There is greatness on the inside of you, and here's the information you have been waiting for to bring that greatness to the surface.

Enough is enough! It's time to roll back the river, push back the tide. You can move every mountain and lay doubt aside. Rise up and *Take It Back!*

Enthusiastically in Him,

Van

Chapter 1

THE HOUR OF DECISION

I call heaven and earth to record this day against
you, that I have set before you life and death, blessing
and cursing: therefore choose life, that both thou and
thy seed may live:

That thou mayst love the Lord thy God, and that
thou mayest obey his voice, and that thou mayest
cleave unto him: for he is thy life, and the length of
thy days: that thou mayest dwell in the land which the
Lord sware unto thy fathers, to Abraham, to Isaac,
and to Jacob, to give them.

Deuteronomy 30:19,20

Are you walking in the land God has given you to possess? Have you chosen life, or are you dying in the circumstances of despair? Are you and your loved ones rejoicing in blessings or weeping over life's curses? Today as you open this book, I challenge you to decide to take back the ground you've lost, because no matter what your biggest problem is today, it has a limited life span.

You may be thinking, *Van, you just don't understand my problem. I feel like I'm dead.* Let me tell you, there was somebody in the Bible like you. His name was Lazarus, and he *was* dead! Now you may be thinking, *but my life stinks*. Well, so did Lazarus. He'd been dead for four days!

If you're thinking about how discouraged you are, just remember, so were Lazarus' family and friends. But four-day dead Lazarus heard the Word of God — a corpse responded to the Word of God. And if God can raise Lazarus from the dead, He can raise you up out of your dead circumstances and give you a breakthrough in whatever area of your life you need it.

Choose Life

Be assured that today is your last day of spiritual mediocrity. God is moving by His Spirit, and He has come to put you over in life, not under, to give you hope beyond the scope of human limitation. He wants to show you that an atmosphere of expectancy is the breeding ground for miracles.

I challenge you to get ready to take back the ground you have lost to the enemy. Second Timothy 3:1 NKJV says, "Know this, that in the last days perilous times will come." Do you believe we are living in the last days? If these are not the last days, these are your only days; and we are living in the perils of perilous times.

As an insurance agent for twenty years, I used to tell my insurance prospects, "You know mortality in America is running one out of one. When they back the hearse up to your front door, they're not making a practice run."

The prospect would say, "You're pressuring me." My response was, "I don't want to pressure you to take this policy. Look it over tonight and then call me in the morning — if you wake up!"

The first year in the insurance business they gave me a rate book and a mirror. The rate book was to figure out how much the policies cost. It soon became clear that the mirror was to watch myself starve to death. Selling furniture supplemented my income during those early days of my career — I sold my couch, my stereo, my TV set. But within five years, I was 517th out of 11,000 agents in the New York Life Insurance Company and became a qualifying member of the Million Dollar Round Table — the President's Council. This produced more money and success at a young age than I knew how to handle.

In the middle of all that, my whole life began falling apart. My home was in crisis. It felt like we were raising the kind of children I didn't want mine to play with. Communication had ceased long ago, and our marriage was dying. In my insurance business, the people that had no intention of paying had quit buying. Times were tough!

If we had met during those years, you would have found me depressed, despondent, and discouraged — those were my strong points. But thanks to the resurrection power of the Lord Jesus Christ, I climbed out of that pit and stayed out by getting into the realm of the Spirit and taking back what the devil had stolen from me all those years. You can do it too!

This book provides you with a number of easy to use, proactive, TT principles that work — that means principles that are "Tried and Tested." No one likes to work with theories. My wife, Doni, and I are living proof that they work, and we're still using them. So can you!

Give the Devil a Wake-up Call

Are you ready to take back what's been stolen from you? Think carefully. Are you ready to put on your battle fatigues, pick up your weapons, and fight for what is rightfully yours? During the battles of life, you will be tempted to withdraw, become timid, and be passive. Don't! Satan is a bully. Bullies delight in shy, timid, wimpy non-fighters. Real fighters intimidate Satan. Whatever Satan confronts you with today, be bold, fight back, and he will flee. James 4:7 says it clearly, "Resist the devil, and he will flee from you." That's right. He's out of there! But the devil *has* to obey the spoken Word of God.

Are you ready to change the way you think, change what you do, and rise up and take a stand instead of just hanging on by your fingernails? If your answer is a sincere and resounding YES, then this is your hour of decision.

What kind of a decision? Only a quality decision produces lasting change. A quality decision is where you and you alone decide to decide. It is that gut-wrenching, all consuming process when you come to the end of yourself and say, "Enough is enough, I can't take it anymore, I'm not going to live this way any longer!" This is your finest hour. The hour you make a "quality decision" in your life.

You're in the right place at the right time. You're receiving breakthrough information. Decide to fly with the eagles rather than to scratch with the chickens. Decide to win and not lose. Decide to succeed and not fail.

Now, go back and read again the foundation scripture for this chapter, Deuteronomy 30:19,20. God is dealing with the children of Israel in this great chapter of restoration. God said to His own children, "Nothing's going to happen until you make a decision." God always gives us a choice and NOW is the time for YOU to choose life and blessings for you and your loved ones. No one can make this choice for you, and no one can take it away from you unless you allow it.

Here are four keys to living a life of blessings: 1) decide to win; 2) don't back down or waver in your decision no matter what; 3) do only what the Word says and say only what the Word says about every situation; and 4) don't ever give up. God wants to heal your spirit, soul, and body. Your healing hinges on your decision.

Decide to Decide

Now you're ready to take the first step and make a quality decision. This is the "want to" step in the process. Start by specifically writing down your quality decision. In doing this, take an inventory of what you have and be sure to use positive wording. Stabilize your present so you can move up to the next level one step at a time.

As a young insurance agent just starting out, I was terribly discouraged. I learned my sales presentation word for word and knew my part. The only problem was, my prospects didn't know their part. At the close of my sales presentation, they just sat there with a glassy-eyed look, not responding at all to my close. Nothing was working. My efforts seemed to be in vain. It was a very difficult time in my life.

After six months of floundering, I collected and studied all of the rules for making the different production clubs at New York Life. I sat down and wrote out a specific goal to qualify for the President's Council of the New York Life Insurance Company.

Breaking the production schedule down month by month and adopting a rule made by one of my mentors, Charles "Tremendous" Jones, to sell at least two policies every week or buy one myself, I committed myself to the business. The first prospect I called on was myself, and I started building my program from there. My own insurance premiums were higher than some people paid on their home mortgage. I became totally and completely committed to the business.

My quality decision was to do whatever it took to qualify for the President's Council, even if it meant working seven days a week, twenty hours a day — no ifs, ands, or buts! No excuses! If I didn't sell a policy for the week, I bought one on my own life. This resulted in ten or twelve policies on my own life worth about a half a million dollars in insurance. The high premiums for these policies forced me to work harder than ever.

My quality decision catapulted me into multimillion dollar production. It caused doors to open up to speak across America to the National Association of Life Underwriters. I did not realize at the time that this quality decision made in the insurance industry would one day propel me towards ministry. It taught me that if you don't run your business like a ministry and your ministry like a business, you won't be in your particular industry very long.

Do Whatever It Takes

Now it's critical to determine the "how to." Until you put feet to what you've decided, nothing will change in your circumstances — because it's not what you know, it's what you *do* about what you know. Decide how you're going to do it and write it all out in simple steps. You may be saying, "But my problem is, I don't know how to do anything about this." Just remember, a vision minus a plan is simply a dream.

If you don't know where to start, then start with God. Make the first "to do" on your list to pray! Use these five prayer requests as a guide: 1) Ask God for whatever you need or want. 2) Ask Him to reveal to you the scriptures on which you need to stand for your circumstances. 3) Ask Him to reveal any areas of unforgiveness or bitterness which need to be dealt with. 4) Ask Him to send the right people across your path to help you make this stand and to remove those people who might be a hindrance to your progress. (5) Ask Him to open the right doors and to provide the resources you need to make possible whatever changes are necessary.

> *Trust in the Lord, and do good; dwell in the land, and feed on His faithfulness.*
> *Delight yourself also in the Lord, and He shall give you the desires of your heart.*
>
> Psalm 37:3,4 NKJV

Seize the Day

With God's help, here are six important steps to help you create your desired future.

STEP ONE: *Focus your thinking.* Determine the specific goals you want to achieve in the next six to twelve months. Be specific. If you can't measure it, how will you ever know if you get there. If you've never set goals before, it might be best to set just one or two to start out. If your quality decision requires more than one goal to be set, break the goals down into small, manageable pieces. The apostle Paul said, "This one thing I do" (Philippians 3:13). He didn't say, "These twenty things I dabbled at." Remember, Rome wasn't built in a day, so don't try to change your whole life overnight. Take it one day at a time.

STEP TWO: *Develop a written plan for achieving each goal and a deadline for its attainment.* Save the hymn, "In the Sweet By and By," for another day. Go back and start with God, praying over each goal and using the five prayer requests we just talked about. Set a deadline that is reasonable and achievable. This will keep you from becoming discouraged.

STEP THREE: *Develop a sincere desire to accomplish the things God has called you to do.* A burning desire is the greatest motivator of every human action. The apostle Paul said, "I press toward the mark for the prize of the high calling of God in Christ Jesus" (Philippians 3:14). Get excited about your own high calling and press toward it.

STEP FOUR: *Continue to develop an unshakable confidence in God.* You ARE what the Bible says you are! You HAVE what the Bible says you have! And you can DO what the Bible says you can do! Find those scriptures that fit your need and stand on them. Speak them out loud frequently. The enemy has to respond to the Word.

STEP FIVE: *Take action and follow through on your plan regardless of obstacles, criticism, circumstances, or what other people say, think, or do.* Utilize sustained effort, controlled attention, and concentrated energy. Don't give up the fight!

Part of this fifth step involves raising your excuse level. I told my son one time, "If 'ifs' and 'buts' were candy and nuts, we'd all have a merry Christmas." Some people spend more time working on excuses than they do on getting the task done. You'll hear people say things like: "The task will take care of itself if I just ignore it long enough. It might be embarrassing. I don't know where to begin. The job's just overwhelming."

Some other excuses you'll hear are, "I'm too tired. I've got to tidy up first." Or, "I need to sleep on it." The list of excuses goes on and on: "There's a good program on TV. I've tried all this before. It just won't work." Raise your excuse level — cut off those excuses.

Here's how to do it. Make a two-column list. On the left, write down the excuses you find yourself using most often or that come to mind as you think about each goal. On the right, write down ways you will overcome each of these excuses with a specific action. For example, if your goal is to read the Word on a daily basis, the excuse on the right might be, "I'm too tired to read my Bible tonight." The overcoming action might be, "I will read my Bible daily for at least five minutes no matter how tired I am."

Progress is being made. You've made a quality decision, you've written it down, and you've written down how you plan to make it happen, including ways to cut off the excuses that might keep you from succeeding.

STEP SIX: *Set a B.A.B. — "Base Acceptable Bottom" — for each of your goals.* Say to yourself, "This is the very least I will do in this specific time frame which I have set for myself." I used to go to meetings and get so depressed. Networking during lunch around the book table, hearing people tell some of the great victories they were having in their lives, made me feel like such a loser. You can't start where someone else is at. You can only start where you're at. Set a base acceptable bottom. Dr. Kenneth Blanchard said it best in *The One Minute Manager*, "People who feel good about themselves produce good results."[1]

When I made my quality decision to become a qualifying member of the President's Council of the New York Life Insurance Company, I set a B.A.B for myself. I committed to complete at least ten contacts with individual prospects per day. This meant I had to call and actually talk to ten individual prospects no matter how many calls it took to do it. Sometimes it took ten calls to reach one person, and it might take as many as thirty to forty calls to reach all ten. By acting on the base acceptable bottom, my production increased and the consistency of my efforts paid off, helping me to reach my goal.

Be a Record Breaker

Go back and look at each of your goals. Set a B.A.B. for each goal as appropriate. Then create a written master checklist of your B.A.B.'s. Why? Because people that break records keep records, and you cannot manage what you cannot measure. As you develop this checklist, break it down into small, measurable steps or tasks. And don't just write down your checklist and stick it in a drawer. Keep it in front of your eyes daily. You can't do it all at once.

Try selecting one, two, or three items from your master checklist each day and write them in your daily planner. Do something from your checklist each day. It feels so good to check off those B.A.B.'s on your list at the end of the day. You've just got to do it. You've got to get started getting started.

It all begins with a quality decision. Take the time to apply the tried and tested principles from this chapter.

Give yourself permission to win and don't back down —
no matter what. Listen to what God is saying to you,
allow His Spirit to lead you, and be proactive. Find your
staying power in God and what Jesus bought for you at
the cross. Then stand firm and take back what rightfully
belongs to you. Remember, today is the first day of the
rest of your life. Make it count!

Meditate on these scriptures:

*I can do all things through Christ who
strengthens me.*

Philippians 4:13 NKJV

Be renewed in the spirit of your mind,

*And that you put on the new man which was
created according to God, in true righteousness
and holiness.*

Ephesians 4:23,24 NKJV

*Be anxious for nothing, but in everything by
prayer and supplication, with thanksgiving, let your
requests be made known to God;*

*And the peace of God, which surpasses all
understanding, will guard your hearts and minds
through Christ Jesus.*

Philippians 4:6,7 NKJV

Q: What quality decision have you made and written down today?

Q: How has writing it down made you see more clearly or changed your focus on the circumstances?

Q: What two excuses will you cut off when writing your "how to" plan?

Q: What is one B.A.B. (base acceptable bottom) you will put on your checklist?

Chapter 2

DON'T BLAME GOD

The thief cometh not, but for to steal, and to kill,
and to destroy: I am come that they might have life,
and that they might have it more abundantly.

John 10:10

Are you fighting the good fight but feel like you are drowning? Have you prayed and prayed and don't see any answers coming your way? Are you at the end of your rope and hanging on for dear life? Is the pain more than you think you can bear? Whatever your situation is today, don't blame God.

"Don't blame God?" you say, "but Van, you don't know what I'm going through!" Maybe I haven't walked in your shoes, but I'm here to tell you today, don't blame God for life's circumstances, what the devil does, or sometimes what you permit! If you believe God's Word is true, then believe all of it, including John 10:10. Jesus came to give us abundant life.

The devil is alive and well in this world today, and he is an expert at robbing us of that abundant life. Despite all the strife and turmoil in today's world, many Bible-believing Christians don't agree with that statement. If you go out and buy George Barna's book,

What Americans Believe, you'll find that out of 10,000 evangelical Christians he surveyed, 47 percent said, "We're not certain whether there is a devil or he's simply a symbol for evil."[1] Here's what God's Word says about such a statement:

> *My people are destroyed for lack of knowledge....*
>
> Hosea 4:6

No wonder so many Christians are being beat up and bloodied. If you don't know you have an enemy, you're already defeated. Don't let the enemy blind your mind. Let your light shine even when it seems like you are in the darkest of circumstances.

> *The god of this age has blinded the minds of unbelievers, so that they cannot see the light of the gospel of the glory of Christ, who is the image of God.*
>
> *For God, who said, "Let light shine out of darkness," made his light shine in our hearts to give us the light of the knowledge of the glory of God in the face of Christ.*
>
> 2 Corinthians 4:4,6 NIV

Not long after Hurricane Andrew tore up southern Florida, I went to South Dade County, Florida, to speak to a large hospital corporation. Before stepping up to the podium, one of the executives took me aside and said, "Now be sensitive, because you'll have people in your audience that an hour before Hurricane Andrew hit had a home. Hours later they had nothing but rubble, with their belongings and furniture scattered all over southern Florida. We have 160,000 people homeless, 28,000 homes destroyed, in excess of $20 billion of damage."

Speaker and teacher, Mike Murdock, says, "When you have nothing left but God, you've got enough to start again." That's exactly what I told that group of people in Florida that day. Well, a fella got up and said, "Yeah, we had an act of God down here." I said, "What?" He said, "Yeah, God blew down a bunch of homes and churches out here in our area." I said, "Well sir, God's not out blowing down churches; He's out putting them up. You've got 'stinkin theological thinkin.' The God I know is a good God, and He's out to put you over, not under."

Enough to Start Again

I don't know what your situation is today, but you're not reading this book by mistake. You have enough to start again. You can make it! Here's how to handle the tragedies and difficult times we face in this world — with the Word of God.

*Giving thanks always for all things unto God and
the Father in the name of our Lord Jesus Christ.*
Ephesians 5:20

Does this mean we are to thank God for the devastation of Hurricane Andrew? Look carefully at the scripture and you will notice it says we are "giving thanks always for all things UNTO GOD." We are to give thanks always for the things God has done — not for what the devil has done.

For example, suppose the doctors tell me I am dying of cancer. I'm not going to thank God for making me sick. I am going to thank God for healing me by His stripes and not accept the devil's bad news. Exodus 15:26 says, "I am the Lord that healeth thee," and Matthew 8:17 says, "Himself took our infirmities, and bare our sicknesses." Praise God, He has made a way for you and me to get out of the bondage of sickness and infirmity.

No Longer a Victim!

We are to give thanks "in" everything because we can take the Word of God and rise above the circumstances. We can stand up to the enemy, put our foot on the necks of Satan and his demons, and cast them out of our circumstances. We can look up, see the open door of God's Word, and march right through that door and out of the circumstances. We don't have to be a victim any longer.

No temptation has seized you except what is common to man. And God is faithful; he will not let you be tempted beyond what you can bear. But when you are tempted, he will also provide a way out so that you can stand up under it.

1 Corinthians 10:13 NIV

Unfortunately, too many times when bad things happen we spend our time wallowing in grief and sorrow instead of looking for God's way out. Just like the man in Florida blamed God for Hurricane Andrew's destruction, we start crying and asking God, "How could You let this happen to me?" (Notice the "me" in that sentence.)

Again we've been duped by the enemy into thinking grief and sorrow are healthy emotions that we just have to work through one step at a time. In actuality, the Word says to "sorrow not." Let's look at 1 Thessalonians 4:13,14.

I would not have you to be ignorant, brethren, concerning them which are asleep, that ye sorrow not, even as others which have no hope.

For if we believe that Jesus died and rose again, even so them also which sleep in Jesus will God bring with him.

There's an old saying, "You can't have your cake and eat it too." As believers, if we have hope in what Jesus did for us on Calvary, we can't have sorrow as well. Extended grief and sorrow are used by the devil to choke the Word of God out of our hearts. The devil gains a foothold when we allow our feelings to rule our circumstances. It is dangerous territory.

We must choose not to succumb to any pressure the devil tries to put on our emotions. If we allow it, the natural emotions of grief and sorrow can hang on longer than is healthy. That's when the enemy slips in with the oppression and heaviness that lead to depression. In Jesus we have victory over sorrow and grief, not just for physical death but in every circumstance.

> *The redeemed of the Lord shall return, and come with singing unto Zion; and everlasting joy shall be upon their head: they shall obtain gladness and joy; and sorrow and mourning shall flee away.*
>
> *Isaiah 51:11*

We are the redeemed of the Lord. We need to stop blaming God when faced with difficult circumstances and start standing on His promises rather than sitting on the premises. We need to get our eyes off the circumstances and back onto our Lord.

O give thanks unto the Lord, for he is good: for his mercy endureth forever.

Let the redeemed of the Lord say so, whom he hath redeemed from the hand of the enemy.

Psalm 107:1,2

I'll never forget the wisdom I learned when I went to a meeting in Chicago to hear a noted theologian. He never made it to the meeting. Instead, he sent a little man from Africa who couldn't even construct a grammatically-correct English sentence.

You say, "Did that bother you?" No, I couldn't either. I was terrible in school. I was in the third of the class that made the upper two-thirds possible, and English was a real struggle for me. My English teacher seemed like such a mean lady — the kind of lady that would sell a seesaw to a hermit! She would come into class and write on the blackboard, "I don't have no fun at the beach," and ask, "How would you correct that?" I said, "Get a boyfriend. Things will pick up for you." (She had no sense of humor either!)

God and the Devil Haven't Traded Places

But that little man from Africa got up and preached for ninety minutes on three points. He preached, "Number one, God is a good God. Number two, the devil, he's a bad devil. Number three, they haven't traded places." Walking out of there that night, my spirit was excited because I knew God was a good God, the devil was a bad devil, and they hadn't traded places. That is a revelation the Body of Christ needs to embrace in these days.

But I carried it too far and became a spiritual Flip Wilson. Comedian Flip Wilson of the 1970s portrayed a character by the name of Geraldine who had a weakness for buying new dresses. Every time she walked by the dress store, the devil began to speak to her. He said, "Geraldine, you might as well go on in. What's a little try-on going to hurt you. You owe yourself a try-on."

She said, "The devil shoved me in that dress store and pushed me up to the counter." Before she knew it, she had bought a new dress. When she got home her husband said, "Geraldine, I thought we agreed together in this household there were not going to be any more new dresses at this time." And Geraldine, in that classic line would say, "Honey, the devil made me buy that dress!"

The Devil Made Me Do It!

Here was a convenient cop-out for all of my lack of diligence and lack of faithfulness. Somebody would say, "Why were you late for the meeting?" I'd say, "The devil made me late." Or they'd say, "Why, we thought you were going to help us usher." I'd say, "The devil detained me." The devil did this; the devil did that. You see, we live in the world and there is a devil. But if I want to live a victorious life, I have a responsibility for dealing with my flesh and doing what I know to do when I know to do it.

I was like the guy out on the construction job. The first day he opened up his lunch and said, "I can't believe it, starting off the week on Monday with peanut butter sandwiches. I hate peanut butter sandwiches."

Tuesday came. At lunch time again, he opened up his lunch bucket. "I'm sick of it." Slamming down the lid, "I can't believe it, peanut butter sandwiches in my lunch two days in a row. I'm sick of peanut butter sandwiches! I hate peanut butter sandwiches! I can't stand peanut butter sandwiches!" His buddy was getting a little tired of this.

The noon whistle blows on Wednesday. His buddy says, "Hey, you want to have a little lunch?"

"Yeah, let's go sit down." Opens up his lunch bucket, takes the foil wrap off his sandwich, "AWWWW!"

His buddy says, "What in the world is wrong with you?"

"Peanut butter sandwiches three days in a row!!!"

"Look, I like having some company at lunch time, but I'm getting a little sick of going through this with you. How long have you been married?"

He said, "Seventeen years."

His buddy says, "What? You mean to tell me after seventeen years, your wife doesn't know that you don't like peanut butter sandwiches?"

He says, "You leave my wife out of this. I pack my own lunch!"

What am I saying? I'm telling you, when you have a problem, you might have brought it on yourself. An old Pogo cartoon once said it like this: "We've met the enemy and it's us!" But who gets the blame? Somebody looked over to the curb and saw the devil crying and said, "Devil, why are you crying?" He said, "All those things the Christians blame me for that I haven't had time to do!"

When I point my finger at God, the devil, or anyone else, there are three fingers pointing right back at me. My friend, Mike Murdock, says, "Don't complain about what you permit!" You and I have a responsibility for taking authority over our flesh, for being diligent and faithful in obeying God's Word, and for walking it out in our lives.

Don't Play Games With the Enemy

If you want to live a victorious life, realize that we live in the world. Satan is the god of this world. God is a good God. The devil is a bad devil, and they haven't switched places. We can't afford to play games with the devil any more. He's real, and he's stealing from us and killing us, and we're letting him do it.

Today is the day to stop blaming God for what the devil does, to use the authority God has given you to defeat the enemy, and to accept responsibility for your own fleshly actions.

Meditate on these scriptures:

In every thing give thanks: for this is the will of God in Christ Jesus concerning you.

1 Thessalonians 5:18

He who does what is sinful is of the devil, because the devil has been sinning from the beginning. The reason the Son of God appeared was to destroy the devil's work.

1 John 3:8 NIV

God is not a man, that he should lie; neither the son of man, that he should repent: hath he said, and shall he not do it? or hath he spoken, and shall he not make it good?

Numbers 23:19

Though I walk in the midst of trouble, thou wilt revive me: thou shalt stretch forth thine hand against the wrath of mine enemies, and thy right hand shall save me.

The Lord will perfect that which concerneth me: thy mercy, O Lord, endureth for ever: forsake not the works of thine own hands.

Psalm 138:7,8

> *Study to shew thyself approved unto God, a workman that needeth not to be ashamed, rightly dividing the word of truth.*
>
> 2 Timothy 2:15

> *The name of the Lord is a strong tower: the righteous runneth into it, and is safe.*
>
> Proverbs 18:10

> *How God anointed Jesus of Nazareth with the Holy Ghost and with power: who went about doing good, and healing all that were oppressed of the devil; for God was with him.*
>
> Acts 10:38

Q: What has happened to you or others when God was blamed for a difficult or tragic situation?

Q: Thinking back on a time when your circumstances seemed impossible or unbearable, what good can you now see that came of it?

Q: What scripture has been a strength and a comfort to you in times of trouble or pain?

Q: What do you plan to do different the next time you find yourself in a difficult situation?

Chapter 3

GET HONEST BEFORE GOD

Have mercy upon me, O God, according to thy lovingkindness: according unto the multitude of thy tender mercies blot out my transgressions.

Wash me throughly from mine iniquity, and cleanse me from my sin.

For I acknowledge my transgressions: and my sin is ever before me.

Psalm 51:1–3

If we truly desire to take back the ground the enemy has stolen and to stop him in his tracks from stealing from us in the future, we must get honest before God. We were all born with a sin nature, but Jesus set us free from that nature on the cross by the shedding of His blood. It is our choice to either walk in the victory of the cross over sin or allow sin to rule us.

For he hath made him to be sin for us, who knew no sin; that we might be made the righteousness of God in him.

2 Corinthians 5:21

David was a man after God's own heart, but he was a man after all. He let down his guard, allowed the lust of the flesh to rule, and opened the door to the enemy. He paid a dear price for his sin with Bathsheba. But in the end he remained humble and honest before the Lord, taking full responsibility for his sin.

You deserve honesty from the heart; yes, utter sincerity and truthfulness. Oh, give me this wisdom.

Psalm 51:6 *TLB*

Sin Is Sin

Unless you and I make a decision to get honest before God, we cannot walk in the victory of the cross. In the past I've gone to God and said, "God, I've got a problem." God said, "You don't have a problem. Up here in heaven we call it sin. It's not a problem — it's sin. It's not an indiscretion — it's sin. It's not just a mistake — it's sin."

I said, "All right God, well, then I will repent." God said, "You're not repenting." I said, "What am I doing?" He said, "You're into remorse." Well, I said, "What's the difference between repenting and remorse?" He said, "You're trying to feel sorry for things you like to do, and in your heart of hearts you have no intention of changing."

You see, I was looking for a painless quick fix and a fast solution without God dealing with the condition of my heart. "Repent" means to turn from sin, to come back up to the highest level. "Repent" means to have a change of mind. You and I have a responsibility to get honest before God.

Let me say something to you: If you're playing around with gambling, drugs, fornication, adultery, homosexuality, pornography, or even calling 1-900-DIAL-A-DEMON (the psychic hot line), you're playing with fire. Although our town of Wheaton, Illinois, has a large number of ministries located there, not everyone is a Christian. We had a psychic operating in our town, but she went out of business about a month ago. It surprised most of us. We thought she would have seen it coming!

While you're sitting here thinking about taking back your ground, you can forget it if you're willfully sinning, because you've opened a door to the enemy. The devil will come in with a spirit of confusion, causing you to make bad decisions. Not only will you not have any increase, you will have a decrease, almost absolutely guaranteed. You're playing with demonic spirits and whistling for the devil to stop by your house.

He that covereth his sins shall not prosper: but whoso confesseth and forsaketh them shall have mercy.
Proverbs 28:13

And don't sit there saying to yourself, "I don't do any of those terrible things." Sin is sin, and we have all sinned.

> *For all have sinned, and come short of the glory of God.*
>
> *Romans 3:23*

God doesn't say one type of sin is worse than any other. Jesus went willingly to the cross and shed His blood to set us free from our sins. Jesus didn't come to condemn but to convict. He doesn't want to condemn us; He wants to set us free. It is only by our acknowledgment and confession of our sin with a repentant heart that He can forgive us.

> *If we confess our sins, he is faithful and just to forgive us our sins, and to cleanse us from all unrighteousness.*
>
> *1 John 1:9*

Different Ways to Confess Sin

There are different ways in which we sin and, therefore, different ways we should make our confession. Your sin may be against God, against another person, or against a group. It is important to confess it and to make things right with God, with individuals, and with the group as it applies to the situation. Always ask the Lord to give you wisdom and guidance as to whom you should confess, how detailed your confession should be, and what you need to do to make things right.[1]

Although it is important to seek forgiveness for our sins, we must be careful how we go about it. A lack of wisdom and sensitivity in this area can cause even more damage than the original offense.

Areas of Caution

Let's examine some areas of caution to exercise when confessing sin. Only confess your sins to God and to people who are directly impacted physically and/or emotionally by the sin. For example, if you reacted in anger and spoke harshly to your brother, you need to ask God and your brother to forgive you. If you were in a bad mood and simply thought bad thoughts against your brother, you should seek forgiveness from God but not from your brother.

Always deal with the most serious sins first. Sometimes (in our minds anyway) it is easier to deal with little "minor" sins rather than with the "bigger" sins. Holding back or procrastinating about dealing with the "bigger" sins allows time for guilt to build up. That guilt attaches itself to the "little" sins and everything gets blown out of proportion. Or sometimes we never get around to asking for forgiveness, and this just opens the door for bitterness to settle in our hearts.

See to it that no one misses the grace of God and that no bitter root grows up to cause trouble and defile many.

Hebrews 12:15 NIV

Keep your confession short and concise. Don't get involved in rehashing all the sordid details of your sin. Doing so just stirs up the pain and offense all over again. It also opens the door for more misunderstandings and conflict.

It is important to clearly identify the actual sin or offense. Sometimes people get angry and flare up at a seemingly silly incident. What they "appear" to be angry about is not the root of the problem. A wife is angry because her husband is late for dinner. But what she is really angry about is his continuous lack of consideration and ungratefulness for what she does for him. If he asks her to forgive him for being late, it's not going to clear the air regarding his ongoing ungratefulness and lack of consideration.

Timing Is Everything

Use wisdom in finding the right time to seek forgiveness. Sometimes a cooling off is needed so anger does not fuel the fire. However, waiting too long or procrastinating over seeking forgiveness opens the door for the enemy to come in and play the offense over in the minds of those involved. It also allows time for rationalization to take place. Then it becomes easier not to seek forgiveness at all. The wisdom of the Word is the best advice possible.

> *"Be angry, and do not sin": do not let the sun go down on your wrath.*
>
> Ephesians 4:26 NKJV

David was a picture of a man getting honest with God when he asked God to give him what he didn't have. In Psalm 51 David said, "Have mercy upon me." He didn't say "us;" he said "me." He said, "Blot out my transgressions. Wash me.... My sin is ever before me.... Purge me with hyssop, and I shall be clean: wash me, and I shall be whiter than snow.... Create in me a clean heart, O God; and renew a right spirit within me."

Repentance Versus Remorse

You may be thinking, *I know I'm a sinner but I don't know what to pray.* Well, here's a good place to start. Pray what David prayed. David had to get honest before God, and so do you and I. And remember, there's a difference between repentance and remorse. Remorse is where I try to feel sorry for the things I like to do. Repentance is where I change my mind so I can change my actions and return to the highest level and live on top with God.

I heard Dr. Myles Munroe describe the word "repent" this way. He said "RE" means return, and "PENT" means to live up on top. Then he asked, "What is the best room in a hotel?" The answer is, "A penthouse." (At the hotel I stayed in the other night, the towels in our room were so big it took me almost fifteen minutes to get them in my suitcase when I was leaving!)

When the devil comes by and says you need to come down and have some "wacky tobaccy," you need a six-pack, you need some videos, or you need to hang out with the old crowd, you can say to the devil, "Listen, I'm penting. I'm living at the highest level. I'm living up on top. I can't come down." Then sing him that line from the old song by Ray Charles, "Hit the road, Jack, and don't you come back no more, no more, no more, no more."

When you pray, you are asking God to give you His perspective and His wisdom. Unconfessed sin is the number one barrier that prevents you from hearing from God. It also causes your heart to condemn you (notice it is your soulish heart, not God, which condemns you). When this happens, you can't approach God, so you start looking for someone else to do your praying for you. You look for alternative solutions to your problems, which leave God out of the picture. You start seeking from man, and who do you think gets in the picture real quick? The accuser, the master at deception, the liar of all liars begins whispering more condemnation in your ear, and things go from bad to worse. Your ears can't hear God when your heart is condemning you.[2]

A number of years ago I was living in a little studio apartment — newly divorced — living alone in a place that was so small, if I had dropped a handkerchief on the floor, I would have had wall-to-wall carpeting. I was defeated in every area of my life.

Someone had sent me a tape by Dr. Ken Stewart titled, "How to Reign in Life." I didn't feel like there was much point in listening to that tape, because the fact was, life was raining on me. I was lonely, feeling defeated, with bills I had no idea how I was going to pay. The children I had just tucked in bed visited me only as the judge had decreed. What did I have to lose by listening?

As I turned on the tape, Dr. Stewart was talking about being more than a conqueror. Reality was, I was more than conquered. Then he said something that impacted and changed my life. He said there are basically only nine things a person needs to know from the Bible. The first three are that we need to learn who our heavenly Father is, what He has, and what He can do. Then we will begin to see the next three things — who we are, what we have, and what we can do.

First John 4:17 says, "...because as he is, so are we in this world." I began to receive the revelation that God didn't send Jesus to get me out of hell and into heaven;

God sent Jesus to get God out of heaven and into me. That's why I had to find out who my heavenly Father was, what He had, and what He could do, so I could see who I am, what I had, and what I could do. Then it became clear what the last three things are — who the enemy is, what he has, and what he can do — and the answer to the last three is, "Nothing unless we let him."

I began to realize I did not get into the situation I was in overnight, and I wasn't going to come out of it overnight. There was a process I had to follow which involved investing the time to renew my mind with God's Word. God has a desire for us to think like He thinks, so we can talk like He talks, and so that we might be able to walk like Jesus walked. There had to be a change in me, and the change had to come from the inside out. This was a new way to think, and I had to learn what it was and how it worked.

I was a very frustrated person because I was attempting to live at one level and feed myself at another level. David said, "Thy word have I hid in mine heart, that I might not sin against thee" (Psalm 119:11). The problem was, spiritually I was on Slimfast. I was not taking in enough of the Word of God to win in the issues of life. I may have had a desire to repent, but I did not have a Word level or Word base that allowed me to walk out the commandments of God. With every promise there's a commandment, and many times I found myself in remorse rather than genuine repentance.

I used to get up and give motivational talks and say, "A man becomes what he thinks about all day long." My wife said, "If that were true, you would have been a woman by the time you were twenty." What I had to do was change what was going on between my ears, and that change only comes from spending time in God's Word. When we get born again, God's Spirit enters our spirit, but our brains go the same old way. What I needed to do to have genuine repentance was to get my brain in line with God's Word and then live it out in my everyday life.

Choose to Humble Yourself

This is why it is so important to continually humble ourselves and ask the Holy Spirit to examine our hearts. When we are prideful, God resists us; but when we humble ourselves before the Lord, then He will lift us up. By confessing our sins, we purify our hearts so we can draw near to God once again.

> *God opposes the proud but gives grace to the humble.*
> *Come near to God and he will come near to you.*
> *Wash your hands, you sinners, and purify your hearts....*
> *Humble yourselves before the Lord, and he will lift you up.*
>
> James 4:6,8,10 NIV

Has there ever been a time when you have done all you can think of to do and you still don't get a release from your sin? Your heart is still convicted. When that happens, the problem is you, not God or His Word. As hard as that may be to hear, believe me, it is true, because Jesus is the same yesterday and today and forever. (See Hebrews 13:8.) If you reach such a roadblock, it is time to do a checkup on your own life. The best way to do this is to examine yourself.

> *For if we would judge ourselves, we should not be judged.*
>
> 1 Corinthians 11:31

Two key areas to examine are unbelief and unforgiveness, which includes forgiving God, forgiving others, AND forgiving yourself. Check out each of these areas of sin in your life and deal with them immediately.

> *For verily I say unto you, That whosoever shall say unto this mountain, Be thou removed, and be thou cast into the sea; and shall not doubt in his heart, but shall believe that those things which he saith shall come to pass; he shall have whatsoever he saith.*

Therefore I say unto you, What things soever ye desire, when ye pray, believe that ye receive them, and ye shall have them.

And when ye stand praying, forgive, if ye have ought against any: that your Father also which is in heaven may forgive you your trespasses.

Mark 11:23–25

God Already Knows

Get honest with God, and if you've missed it, tell Him you've missed it. God knew Hitler. He knew Atilla the Hun. He knew John Dillinger. You're not some VIP sinner. God is impressed when you take the time to be honest before Him and let Him deal with the condition of your heart. He won't be surprised. He already knows about it. He has just been waiting for you to be honest with Him. Then and only then can you walk in the victory of the cross and operate in the authority He has given you.

Meditate on these scriptures:

Search me, O God, and know my heart: try me, and know my thoughts:

And see if there be any wicked way in me, and lead me in the way everlasting.

Psalm 139:23,24

And it shall come to pass, if thou shalt hearken diligently unto the voice of the Lord thy God, to observe and to do all his commandments which I command thee this day, that the Lord thy God will set thee on high above all nations of the earth:

And all these blessings shall come on thee, and overtake thee, if thou shalt hearken unto the voice of the Lord thy God.

Deuteronomy 28:1,2

Finally, brethren, whatsoever things are true, whatsoever things are honest, whatsoever things are just, whatsoever things are pure, whatsoever things are lovely, whatsoever things are of good report; if there be any virtue, and if there be any praise, think on these things.

Philippians 4:8

There is therefore now no condemnation to them which are in Christ Jesus, who walk not after the flesh, but after the Spirit.

For the law of the Spirit of life in Christ Jesus hath made me free from the law of sin and death.

Romans 8:1,2

Q: What experience clearly stands out in your mind when you offended someone and had to ask for forgiveness?

Q: How did they respond to you?

Q: How did it make you feel?

Q: What will you do differently the next time you are faced with such a situation?

Chapter 4

DO WHAT'S RIGHT!

*And if I say to the wicked man, "You will surely
die," but he turns away from his sin and does what is
just and right — if he gives back what he took in
pledge for a loan, returns what he has stolen, follows
the decrees that give life, and does no evil, he will
surely live; he will not die.*

*None of the sins he has committed will be
remembered against him. He has done what is just
and right; he will surely live.*

Ezekiel 33:14–16 NIV

We talked about the importance of confessing and
repenting of our sins — truly turning away from sin and
having a change of heart. But as we read in the above
passage of Scripture, we see there is more involved in the
forgiveness process. We must 1) turn away from the sin
(that means stop doing it), 2) do what is just and right,
3) give back what is taken in pledge for a loan, 4) return
anything that is stolen, and 5) live a righteous life in
obedience to God's principles.[1] We must do what's right
and be willing to make amends and restitution to those
we have wronged if we want to be blessed and walk in a
life of increase instead of decrease.

War Against the Flesh

Let me make a statement about sin that is theologically correct. When you come to Christ, your sin is all under the blood of Jesus, but you still war against the flesh. Paul addresses this in his letter to the Romans.

> For I delight in the law of God after the inward man:
> But I see another law in my members, warring
> against the law of my mind, and bringing me into
> captivity to the law of sin which is in my members.
>
> Romans 7:22,23

I visited a church one time and met a forty-something man and his forty-year-old wife. I went back to that church six months later and met the same man. This time he was standing there with some gal who looked like his niece. I said, "How's the missus?" He said, "Ho, Ho, Ho, Ho, Glory to God! Yes! Hallelujah! Well, after sixteen years of marriage, we found out that we just weren't compatible. Now we do have three children, but hey, I've got to find myself. And we just didn't love each other anymore."

I said, "Well now, brother, was there any hope for reconciliation...could you work...was there any chance...?"

"Aww, no, no, ah, it's just all under the blood. We just had to go our separate ways."

When some men get about forty-something, they begin to act like they are brain damaged and want to trade in their forty-year-old wife for two twenties. Let me tell you something, men. When you're forty-something, you're not wired for two twenties. So forget it.

Paul goes on to say in Romans that we cannot live according to the flesh and please God. We can't walk in the flesh and the Spirit at the same time. Sin is sin, and our Father is not going to look the other way! Therefore, being under the blood of Jesus does not give us freedom to walk in the flesh, according to the world's standards. We must walk according to the Spirit to have life.

This man was deceived. He was walking in the flesh and thinking he was protected under the blood. He has already paid a price by losing his wife and family. Unless he repents and does what is just and right, the enemy will continue to rob, steal, and destroy his life.

> *For those who live according to the flesh set their minds on the things of the flesh, but those who live according to the Spirit, the things of the Spirit.*
>
> *For to be carnally minded is death, but to be spiritually minded is life and peace.*
>
> *So then, those who are in the flesh cannot please God.*
>
> *Romans 8:5,6,8 NKJV*

Sometimes we do things very innocently and don't think about how our actions affect our testimony to others. But God sees it for what it is — sin. One night while walking through my garage, I looked up and spotted a rake hanging on the wall. God said, "Whose rake is that?" I said, "The man's down the street." God said, "When were you planning on returning it?" I said, "Well, I told him I'd have it back by Saturday night."

God said, "That was Saturday night a month ago. You've got a problem. Your word is no good. Your yes is not yes, and your no is not no! I am a convenant-keeping, word-keeping God. I keep My Word. You call yourself a Christian. You need to either change your conduct or change your name!" God convicted me. I had to confess my sin to Him, and I had to make things right with my neighbor.

Let Your Yes be Yes

We want to have financial increase, but we make up stories for our creditors, and we make up stories with others when we do something that's not quite right. We want victory in our lives instead of defeat, but our word is no good. We need to be diligent in all things, big and small.

Have you ever given a set of tapes to a recovering drug addict and told him you need it back in two weeks? On Friday night in the middle of a rainstorm, a knock comes on the door, and the guy says, "Here's your tapes." But loan them to a fellow Christian, and you might as well put some mistletoe around them and kiss them good-bye.

Have you ever lent money to a Christian brother? On Sunday morning you say, "Hey, look, God just showed me you need some money. Here's twenty dollars." He says, "Oh, no, no, no, no. Well, hey, I could use it, but Friday night in the prayer service I'll have it back to you. I'll see you then. I'll see you and get it right back to you Friday night."

Friday night comes. You sit here; he sits there right across the aisle. The twenty dollars never comes up in the conversation. Sunday morning comes. You sit here; he sits there in your usual seats. The next Sunday comes and goes and nothing is said. You wouldn't have minded giving him the twenty dollars, but he insisted he wanted to pay you back. You'd just like to bring it to closure, because you don't want twenty dollars to put a wedge in the middle of your relationship.

You try to think of creative ways to find out if you're getting your money back. In the middle of a praise and worship service, the praise leader is singing, "God's a God of plenty." You slide over by your friend and sing, "Do you have my twenty?"

One Board at a Time

If you want to live victoriously, you've got to be willing to make amends and restitution and do it with your whole heart — not like the man that got a job at a lumberyard. The first day he was there, he took one little piece of lumber home to fix a broken fence. The next day, he took another piece for a little fix-it project, then another and another. He became one of the most prosperous men in his town, and his church wanted to make him a deacon.

Well, he got to feeling guilty about what he'd been doing all these years. He thought, *I've got to talk to somebody. I've got to go to my pastor and make things right.* Then he thought about it some more. *No, that pastor of mine is probably a pretty straight shooter. He might even call the sheriff and have me arrested. Who can I go to? I know what I'll do. I've got a Catholic friend. He goes to something called confession. I'm going to go down and see the priest and see if I can go to confession. Then I'll feel better.*

He drives down to the Catholic church and says, "Father, I'm a Protestant, but could I come and talk to you?" The priest said, "Well, of course, you can. There are a lot of Protestants that ought to be down here talking to me." He said, "Well, you've got this thing called confession. Could I go to that?" The priest said, "Well, I don't see what would be wrong with that."

So he goes in and confesses what he had been doing. About thirty minutes later, he walks out and says, "Father, hallelujah, I feel so much better. I didn't realize that's all there was to it. Just come in there and say a few words, tell you what I've been doing, have a prayer, and go on my merry way."

The priest said, "Get back here." The man asked, "What's the problem?" The priest said, "You don't do that. You don't just come in here and confess to me and say a prayer and go on your merry way. You need to make restitution. Now, son, let me ask you something. Have you ever made a novena?" The man said, "No, but if you can get the plans, I can probably get the lumber."

An Attitude of the Heart

Don't laugh. That's the way a lot of people approach their sin. But you say, "What's the big deal?" Listen, here's the big deal. Confessing sin with your mouth and not changing in your heart is not repentance.

If you try to take back the ground that has been stolen from you with this kind of an attitude, the devil will tell you all the reasons that you're not qualified to have that ground. He'll use that broken relationship and the bitterness you hold in your heart, those unkind words spoken in anger, that unreturned rake, the tools you took home from work, and the tape set you borrowed and never returned to bring condemnation into your life and to hold you back from living a life of blessing.

If you get honest before God, make things right with God and those involved, and then make amends and restitution, the devil will not be able to hold you in bondage any longer. One way to test your motives is to ask yourself this question, "Will what I am about to do build my confidence with God?" Consider what the Word says,

> *Dear friends, if our hearts do not condemn us,*
> *we have confidence before God*
> *And receive from him anything we ask, because*
> *we obey his commands and do what pleases him.*
> 1 John 3:21,22 NIV

The Power of a Clear Conscience

This is so important, let's consider some additional scriptures which confirm the power of a clear conscience as it affects our testimony.

> *And herein do I exercise myself, to have always*
> *a conscience void of offense toward God, and*
> *toward men.*
> Acts 24:16

> *For our rejoicing is this, the testimony of our*
> *conscience, that in simplicity and godly sincerity, not*
> *with fleshly wisdom, but by the grace of God, we*

have had our conversation in the world, and more
abundantly to you-ward.

2 Corinthians 1:12

Having a good conscience; that, whereas they
speak evil of you, as of evildoers, they may be ashamed
that falsely accuse your good conversation in Christ.

1 Peter 3:16

Paul speaks to Timothy about a clear conscience
actually being a weapon of war.

This charge I commit unto thee, son Timothy,…
that thou by them mightest war a good warfare;
Holding faith, and a good conscience; which
some having put away concerning faith have made
shipwreck.

1 Timothy 1:18,19

Besides the boldness to witness to others, additional
benefits of having a clear conscience include freedom to
resolve conflict, alertness to make wise decisions without
fear of the consequences, the power to overcome temptation and not allow temporary pleasures to draw us into
deeper sin, the ability to build genuine relationships, and
some unexpected bonuses as promised in Proverbs 28:13.[2]

> *He that covereth his sins shall not prosper: but whoso confesseth and forsaketh them shall have mercy.*

Sometimes we have covered our own sins for so long that we can't see the wrongs we have done to others. Our conscience may try to prick us from time to time, but we have rationalized away our own guilt by laying the blame onto others. The longer we allow this to happen, the more dangerous it becomes. We fall into deception, and anger and bitterness have their way in our hearts. James addresses this so clearly when he says,

> *Everyone should be quick to listen, slow to speak and slow to become angry,*
>
> *For man's anger does not bring about the righteous life that God desires.*
>
> *Therefore, get rid of all moral filth and the evil that is so prevalent and humbly accept the word planted in you, which can save you.*
>
> *Do not merely listen to the word, and so deceive yourselves. Do what it says.*
>
> *Anyone who listens to the word but does not do what it says is like a man who looks at his face in a mirror*
>
> *And, after looking at himself, goes away and immediately forgets what he looks like.*

*But the man who looks intently into the perfect
law that gives freedom, and continues to do this, not
forgetting what he has heard, but doing it — he will
be blessed in what he does.*

James 1:19–25 NIV

Take the time to go back and examine your own
heart. Pray and ask the Lord to bring back to your
remembrance any offenses against others or sins you have
buried or rationalized and not made right. Write down
what the Lord shows you and prioritize the list in order of
the seriousness of the offense. Then "do" whatever is
necessary to make things right according to God's Word.[3]

Seek forgiveness from those you have wronged, either
face to face or by telephone. Make amends or restitution
for anything you have taken from others, no matter how
long ago it happened. Don't let pride stand in your way.
Humble yourself and only address what you did wrong,
not what anyone else did. Pray and ask the Lord to give
you wisdom about choosing the right words to speak, the
best method for asking for forgiveness, the right timing,
and for the grace to remain humble and loving regardless
of the other person's reaction.

An acquaintance shared this story with me that
speaks so loudly about the importance of seeking
forgiveness and God's timing. This man was the CEO of

a well-known company and had been very successful in business. Although he had given his life to Jesus as a young boy, he had walked a slippery path of sin for many years thereafter. He had come back to the Lord at the age of forty, but there was a root of bitterness that was hidden deep within his soul.

His father had been a soldier in World War II and had been sent overseas when he was too small to remember him. He had been raised by a loving mother and grandmother. When his father returned from the war, he was seven years old and deeply resented the intrusion of this stranger into his already structured life, where he had been the "man of the house." His father was a strict disciplinarian, and true to his generation, he was never able to show his emotions or express his love to his son.

This man judged his father and held unforgiveness in his heart for what he "perceived" as the harshness with which he was disciplined and the absence of love. As a result, he put up a wall around himself, which no one was allowed to penetrate — even his own wife and children.

The years went by. Then one day he got a call that his father was in the hospital, dying. His father was asking to see him. When he got to the hospital, his father tearfully told him how much he loved him and how proud he was of him. The walls suddenly came tumbling down, and both father and son forgave each other and repented.

The next couple of weeks were precious as father and son shared forty years of their hurts, their dreams, and their joys with each other. This man is forever grateful for those few weeks before his father died. His life was changed forever. He came to realize how wrong he had been about his father and how he had wronged his own children in a similar way.

There was healing in the entire family as he sought their forgiveness as well. His only regret is what could have been if he hadn't believed the lies the enemy planted in his heart as a little boy. These lies became seed for a lifetime of bitterness, and he wondered what might have been had he not allowed his pride to prevent him from seeking his father's forgiveness sooner.

Thank God for His goodness and mercy. When you have a clear conscience before God, you are positioned to go onward and upward. So, do what is right in God's eyes, and discover the freedom and joy that are yours when you walk in obedience to His Word.

Meditate on these scriptures:

Confess your sins to each other and pray for each other so that you may be healed. The prayer of a righteous man is powerful and effective.

James 5:16 NIV

Therefore, if you are offering your gift at the altar and there remember that your brother has something against you,

Leave your gift there in front of the altar. First go and be reconciled to your brother; then come and offer your gift.

Matthew 5:23,24 NIV

Accept one another, then, just as Christ accepted you, in order to bring praise to God.

Romans 15:7 NIV

If anyone would come after me, he must deny himself and take up his cross daily and follow me.

Luke 9:23 NIV

Let no corrupt communication proceed out of your mouth, but that which is good to the use of edifying, that it may minister grace unto the hearers.

Ephesians 4:29

Q: What is one incident in which you don't have a clear conscience?

Q: Are you willing to humble yourself to ask forgiveness, regardless of who was at fault?

Q: What steps must be taken to make things right?

Chapter 5

DEVELOP A NEW FOCUS

Set your mind on things above, not on things on the earth.

For you died, and your life is hidden with Christ in God.

Colossians 3:2,3 NKJV

If you want to take back the ground and possess the land God has given to you, start by developing a new focus. That means, get your mind off the problems or circumstances in your life and onto the solution. Change your thinking from defeat to victory.

Jesus' Focus Changed

Just take a look at the life and ministry of the Lord Jesus Christ and consider how the focus of His ministry changes from Matthew to Revelation. In the gospels, His enemies mock Him — in Revelation, they bow down to Him. In the gospels, He comes to convict sinners — in Revelation, He comes to condemn His enemies. In the gospels, He is pierced — in Revelation, He is praised. In the gospels, He is seen as a victim — in Revelation, He returns as the victor. In the gospels, He wears a crown of thorns — in Revelation, He wears a crown of glory. In the gospels, we see Him hanging on the cross — in Revelation, we see Him charging on a white horse. In the gospels, He dies like a criminal — in Revelation, He returns as a conqueror. In the gospels, He defeats death — in Revelation, He destroys death.

Look at His life — born in poverty, in a smelly barn in a dusty little town of no consequence. That's not the way I'd have done it if I were God. I'd have called ABC, CBS, NBC, "Larry King Live," and CNN, and said, "Hey, the King of kings and the Lord of lords is coming to planet earth." So, who does God tell that Jesus is coming to earth? The lowest socioeconomic group of its day — the shepherds. Not only was it the lowest socioeconomic group of that day, it was the night crew — the eleven–to–seven shift.

God's Ways Are Higher

You may think you're going down, when the fact of the matter is, you're on the way up. Your perspective on the problem may be wrong. You need to get a new perspective. Like I said, I wouldn't have done it like God. But God doesn't think the way we think or do things the way we do them. His ways are higher, and we need to become more like Him.

"For My thoughts are not your thoughts, nor are your ways My ways," says the Lord.

For as the heavens are higher than the earth, so are My ways higher than your ways, and My thoughts than your thoughts.

Isaiah 55:8,9 NKJV

Born in poverty, raised in obscurity, we don't know much about Jesus' life as He was growing up. But whenever Joseph was in the middle of a rehab project, putting up some drywall in a place somewhere around Nazareth, he'd go looking for Jesus. He'd find Him up at the temple, talking with the scholars, getting information, preparing for His future. He was growing in the nurture and admonition of the Lord.

Jesus Had a Sense of Humor

I believe Jesus had a sense of humor, and He enjoyed those trips. I believe those guys looked over and saw Him and said, "Hey, young fella. Hey, boy, You, young fella, the one with all the light around ya, who are You?" I can see Jesus deciding to have a little fun. "Who, Me?"

"Yeah, You."

"Well, on My mother's side they call Me Jesus. But, now on My Father's side, they call Me Emmanuel, God with us."

"What? What kind of answer is that? How old are You?"

"Well, on My mother's side I'm twelve, but on My Daddy's, I'm from eternity past to eternity future."

"We've never heard such a thing. Where are You from anyway?"

"Well, on My mother's side I'm from Bethlehem, the city of David, the house of bread, but on My Father's side I've come from the very portals of heaven."

"That's the craziest thing You've said yet, young fella. What kind of plans do You have?"

"Well, on My mother's side one day out on a hill called Golgotha, the place of the skull, I'm going to die like a common thief for the sins of mankind, but now, on My Daddy's side, I've got another set of plans. After they kill Me, the first thing I plan to do is borrow Me a grave."

"Ha, Ha, that's what we thought. Your family's so poor You can't even afford a grave."

"No," He said, "there's no point in Me making any long-term capital investment in a grave site 'cause I'm only going to need it for about three days. You see, after three days, I plan on busting up out of there with the keys to death, hell, and the grave. I'm going to step on a cloud of shekinah glory, ride on up, and sit down at the right hand of My Father.

"Then one day My Daddy's going to give Me a knowing nod, and I'm going to put My long, lean Galilean leg across the back of a steaming white stallion and ride through the sapphire seals of heaven's gates. I'll begin My march toward the Valley of Megiddo, and they'll write over Me 'King of kings and Lord of lords.' That's Who I Am!"

Christ IN You

That's Who He is. He's the key to your future. When you discover that God didn't send Jesus simply to get you out of hell and into heaven but to get God out of heaven and into you, and you become God-inside-minded, what a difference that will make. When you know Who He is, what He has, and what He can do; you begin to see who you are, what you have, and what you can do. Christ, the Anointed One, lives in you. When you get that truth down inside your very being, you have discovered the mystery of the ages Paul describes in Colossians.

> *The mystery which has been hidden from ages and from generations, but now has been revealed to His saints.*
> *To them God willed to make known what are the riches of the glory of this mystery among the Gentiles: which is Christ in you, the hope of glory.*
> *Colossians 1:26,27 NKJV*

Born in poverty and raised in obscurity, His ministry faced hostility. His suffering was marked by agony. His death was marked by ignominy. His resurrection was marked by victory, and His ascension was marked by majesty. And He did it all for you and for me. So, embrace all He has done for you, accept who you are IN HIM, and watch your focus rise to the level at which God means for His children to walk in this life.

> *As you have therefore received Christ Jesus the Lord, so walk in Him,*
>
> *Rooted and built up in Him and established in the faith, as you have been taught, abounding in it with thanksgiving.*
>
> *For in Him dwells all the fullness of the Godhead bodily; and you are complete in Him, who is the head of all principality and power.*
>
> Colossians 2:6,7,9,10 NKJV

Seated at His Right Hand

King Jesus is on the throne, and the Victor lives in you and me, seated at the right hand of the Father until we exercise His authority to make His enemies His footstool. We must activate the victory of the cross and become the overcomers we are meant to be. Jesus won the victory, but we are here to defend and enforce it. We are to be God's army on this earth. That is why the enemy fights so hard to keep us living in defeat. We define spiritual warfare as what the devil is doing to us, when it should be what we are doing to the devil![1]

Your Mind Is the Battleground

The primary battle we fight is in our minds. The devil loves to whisper thoughts of fear and defeat into our minds. Those fiery darts go into our minds, and as long as we allow him to lie to us, we will not live in victory. We must bring every thought captive that doesn't come from God and cast down every argument. We don't need to argue with the devil. We need to renew our minds and speak the Word with our mouths.

Remember, this is war! Be aggressive and stand up and fight with the weapons God has given you. Don't yield one inch. You have the power of the anointing and the victory of the cross living within you. Your weapons are mighty to the pulling down of strongholds (patterns of thinking contrary to the Word of God that continually give the enemy legal ground to torment and enslave you).[2]

> For though we walk in the flesh, we do not war according to the flesh.
>
> For the weapons of our warfare are not carnal but mighty in God for pulling down strongholds,
>
> Casting down arguments and every high thing that exalts itself against the knowledge of God, bringing every thought into captivity to the obedience of Christ,

*And being ready to punish all disobedience when
your obedience is fulfilled.*

                                        2 Corinthians 10:3–6

There are so many scriptures that build you up in your
mind and fill you to overflowing with who you are in
Christ. Get into the Word and get those nuggets of wisdom
down into your spirit. No matter what your circumstances,
the Word never changes. Here are just a few, and there are
more to meditate on at the end of this chapter.

*For to be carnally minded is death, but to be
spiritually minded is life and peace.*

                                        Romans 8:6 NKJV

*Yet in all these things we are more than
conquerors through Him who loved us.*

                                        Romans 8:37 NKJV

Don't Let the Enemy Steal Your Joy

Anyone who knows me, knows how much I love a
good joke. Laughter has carried me over many hard places
in my life. I believe it truly is better to laugh than to cry,
and the Scriptures clearly reveal that joy is a powerful
spiritual force, a weapon that stops Satan in his tracks. If
we are to be obedient in all things, we must not allow the

enemy to steal our joy. The Lord assures us we will have peace in Him even though we live in a fallen world filled with trials and troubles. The key is to find our joy in knowing He has already overcome the world. Therefore, we are to rejoice in knowing what He has done for us.

These things I have spoken to you, that in Me you may have peace. In the world you will have tribulation; but be of good cheer, I have overcome the world.

John 16:33 NKJV

This day is sacred to our Lord. Do not grieve, for the joy of the Lord is your strength.

Nehemiah 8:10 NIV

Many sorrows shall be to the wicked; but he who trusts in the Lord, mercy shall surround him.

Be glad in the Lord and rejoice, you righteous; and shout for joy, all you upright in heart!

Psalm 32:10,11 NKJV

A merry heart does good, like medicine, But a broken spirit dries the bones.

Proverbs 17:22 NKJV

A few years ago while preparing for a speaking engagement for Mercy Ministries, I opened up my file and to my horror discovered it was a home for unwed mothers. My mind said, *God, what have I gone and done. I'm not qualified to speak to this group, and don't know what to say to them. God, You've got to help me.*

I got my Bible out and began to search for a message. I started with Adam and Eve, Abraham, Isaac, Jacob, Ruth, Esther. Then I moved on to the New Testament with the parable of the ten virgins. But I decided that probably wouldn't go over too big. No message jumped out at me. I said, "God, give me an idea."

Right there in the middle of all that, God gave me an idea. While reading *USA Today*, my eye caught an article about the Barbie Doll, and my spirit leaped within me. (Did you know the Barbie doll line is selling so well, last year they came out with a divorced Barbie? It comes with all Ken's stuff!)

The Barbie Doll Message

Here's my message to that group: "Ladies, first of all, I want to congratulate you on your incredible courage. You're facing adversity. Life is not going to be easy because of what has happened to you, but God will help you. God is here with you, and He has promised He will never leave you nor forsake you. I thank God you chose life rather than death.

"Hey, listen, America aborts 4,500 babies a day, pulling them out of their mother's wombs, and there's not a ten-cent penalty for doing it. But if you destroy, accidentally or on purpose, the egg of a baby eagle, there's a $5,000 fine. Ladies, I want to thank you for your incredible courage. You've chosen life over death.

"Speaking as a former fetus myself, I'm so thankful that my mother was pro-life and didn't drown me in saline solution. Aren't you glad that Joseph and Mary were pro-life? Joseph didn't drag Mary down to Planned Parenthood and try to terminate the birth of the Lord Jesus Christ.

"Let me ask you a question. As young ladies, how many of you owned a Barbie Doll?" Out of twelve women in that room, ten hands went up. Then I said, "Now understand, when your parents gave it to you, they were attempting to bless you, but they didn't know what they were doing. There you were on Christmas morning. You took off the bow, unwrapped the box, and out comes Barbie. Boy, you were excited. Just what you wanted. A Barbie just like all your friends have." They all nodded their heads in agreement.

I went on and said, "Now Barbie's only fourteen or fifteen years of age, but at age fifteen, she has a fully developed woman's figure, incredible long blond hair that floats down her back where it meets — not her Wranglers or Levis, but French designer jeans. She has beautiful blue eyes, sparkling teeth. (Not like mine. I went in to see my dentist and said, 'What would you recommend for yellow teeth?' He said, 'A brown tie would probably go well.') And there are three words that are not in her teenage vocabulary: acne, zit, or Clearasil. Is this any teenager you know?" They all emphatically answered, "No!"

I asked, "Who does Barbie date?" Of course they answered, "Ken." I said, "Now Ken is only seventeen. He's got a twenty-one-inch neck and nineteen-inch biceps. (Reminds me a lot of myself. I went into the Chicago Health Club and said, 'What would you recommend for me?' They said, 'The intensive care unit over at the hospital.') Barbie dates Ken. Ken has a 4X4 that he owns free and clear at age seventeen. He bench presses it when Barbie's not riding around with him."

And I asked these young unwed mothers, "What happens when you look at Barbie and go over to the mirror and look at yourself?" They answered laughing but with sadness in their eyes, "What happened to me? Why don't I look anything like Barbie?" I said, "You see, the world has sold you a bill of goods that the standard of success is the Barbie look, but it's a lie. You look like God made you, and you look good to God.

"Ladies, do you know three words that women hate to hear from men who don't know their meaning but who will use them to get whatever they want?" They said, "What are they?" I said, "It's the words, 'I love you.'" They said, "Yeah, we've heard that before." I said, "You know another thing that women learn real early in life?" They said, "What is that?" I said, "That men lie." They said, "Yeah, they do, don't they."

I said, "Well, I know somebody Who said He loves you, and He never ever did tell a lie. His name's Jesus of Nazareth. If, while you're here at Mercy Ministries, you'll trade in your life to receive His life, and fill yourself up with His realities, His life, you'll never sit here wondering, 'Will I ever have somebody that will cherish me and nourish me and be a husband to me?' Instead you'll sit here and say, 'I wonder who's going to qualify as a mate for me because I am highly favored among women. I've got the life of God in me. I've been made worthy by the Most High and Living God. I'm somebody in God.'"

That message changed the lives of those young unwed mothers. When I didn't think I had anything to share with them, God changed my focus and helped me reach them where they were at. He was faithful. Imagine a Barbie Doll message! He does have a sense of humor.

Keep Your Eyes on the Solution

Whatever your circumstances are, God already knows your need. The key is to keep your eyes on Him. Let Him change your focus, or bring your focus to a higher level.

Remember when Peter got out of the boat and walked on the water to go to Jesus. It was only when he took his eyes off Jesus that he began to sink. He looked at the circumstances around him and doubted.

Jesus is the solution to all your circumstances. Submit to Him and to His Word and then act on what He shows you. You're only one word or one idea away from an incredible future.

When you change your focus, get your mind off your problem and onto the solution — Jesus Christ — you're headed for the top. Know who God says you are. Give up your small ambitions and go to the next level in God. Raise your thinking, and see yourself achieving and going someplace to make something happen.

Meditate on these scriptures:

> *Do not let this Book of the Law depart from your mouth; meditate on it day and night, so that you may be careful to do everything written in it. Then you will be prosperous and successful.*
>
> Joshua 1:8 NIV

> *The lamp of the body is the eye. Therefore, when your eye is good, your whole body also is full of light. But when your eye is bad, your body also is full of darkness.*

If then your whole body is full of light, having no part dark, the whole body will be full of light, as when the bright shining of a lamp gives you light.

Luke 11:34,36 NKJV

More than that, blessed are those who hear the word of God and keep it!

Luke 11:28 NKJV

With men this is impossible, but with God all things are possible.

Matthew 19:26 NKJV

And we, who with unveiled faces all reflect the Lord's glory, are being transformed into his likeness with ever-increasing glory, which comes from the Lord, who is the Spirit.

2 Corinthians 3:18 NIV

Therefore do not cast away your confidence, which has great reward.

For you have need of endurance, so that after you have done the will of God, you may receive the promise.

Hebrews 10:35,36 NKJV

For we do not have a High Priest who cannot sympathize with our weaknesses, but was in all points tempted as we are, yet without sin.

Let us therefore come boldly to the throne of grace, that we may obtain mercy and find grace to help in time of need.

Hebrews 4:15,16 NKJV

Many are the afflictions of the righteous, but the Lord delivers him out of them all.

Psalm 34:19 NKJV

My brethren, count it all joy when you fall into various trials.

James 1:2 NKJV

Every good gift and every perfect gift is from above, and comes down from the Father of lights, with whom there is no variation or shadow of turning.

James 1:17 NKJV

And so we know and rely on the love God has for us. God is love. Whoever lives in love lives in God, and God in him.

In this way, love is made complete among us so that we will have confidence on the day of judgment, because in this world we are like him.

1 John 4:16,17 NIV

Q: How do you need to change your focus?

Q: What fiery darts (thoughts of doubt, unbelief, condemnation, fear, etc.) has the enemy been firing into your mind lately?

Q: Think of one situation when you discovered God's ways were higher or better than your ways?

Chapter 6

LEARN HOW TO RESIST THE DEVIL

*Submit yourselves therefore to God. Resist the
devil, and he will flee from you.*

James 4:7

Have you been resisting the devil with all your might
and feel like the battle just gets hotter with no end in
sight? Are you tired of losing more ground than you gain?
Maybe you're sitting there thinking, *Yeah, been
there...done that!* Well, I found out that resisting the devil
does not start with resist. It starts with submit, and the
more we submit to the Lord, the more we position
ourselves to resist effectively. Then and only then do we
see the devil flee.

Here's what I'm saying: I do a lot of traveling. In the
hotels they've got those movie rental boxes in each room.
Let's see, you can get G for garbage, PG that's for pure
garbage parents should view first, R for rotten, and X for
poison. Well, let's say I call down to the front desk, and
say, "There's a little boy staying in this room — could
manifest in me anytime. Now if he should attempt to try
to come out, I want to make sure all the movie channels
are blocked and none of them work. I don't want any of
that on my TV set!"

There's a Time to Flee

Most people would laugh and say that's crazy. But if more people would be honest with themselves and take such precautions against temptation, they would be much more successful in resisting what the enemy puts in front of them.

If you're a recovering alcoholic, your first witnessing trip doesn't have to be to the local bar. If you're coming out of drugs, don't make your first witnessing trip to a party where everyone is sniffing cocaine. Listen, there's a time to stand, and having done all, to stand. But I want to tell you, there's also a time to flee.

Now hear what I'm saying. I'm not saying there is ever a time to flee from the enemy in fear. I am saying until you are strong enough in your body, soul, and spirit to withstand the temptations the enemy puts in front of you, it is wise to remove yourself out of harm's way.

Learn From the Master

You and I need to learn how to resist the devil, and what better way than to learn from the Master. Jesus showed us a clear picture how to do this at the very beginning of His ministry.

Then Jesus came from Galilee to the Jordan to be baptized by John. But John tried to deter him, saying, "I need to be baptized by you, and do you come to me?"

*Jesus replied, "Let it be so now; it is proper for us to
do this to fulfill all righteousness." Then John consented.*

*As soon as Jesus was baptized, he went up out of
the water. At that moment heaven was opened, and
he saw the Spirit of God descending like a dove and
lighting on him.*

*And a voice from heaven said, "This is my Son,
whom I love; with him I am well pleased."*

Matthew 3:13-17 NIV

Jesus humbled Himself by coming to earth as a man to
live and to die for us sinners. He submitted in obedience
and showed honor to His heavenly Father and His earthly
parents. He did what was right. He was patient to wait
upon His Father's timing (thirty years before beginning
His ministry). He knew the significance and necessity of
water baptism and baptism by the Spirit and its power.

*Then Jesus was led by the Spirit into the desert to
be tempted by the devil.*

*After fasting forty days and forty nights, he
was hungry.*

*The tempter came to him and said, "If you are
the Son of God, tell these stones to become bread."*

Jesus answered, "It is written: 'Man does not live on bread alone, but on every word that comes from the mouth of God."

Then the devil took him to the holy city and had him stand on the highest point of the temple.

"If you are the Son of God," he said, "throw yourself down. For it is written: 'He will command his angels concerning you, and they will lift you up in their hands, so that you will not strike your foot against a stone.'"

Jesus answered him, "It is also written: 'Do not put the Lord your God to the test.'"

Again, the devil took him to a very high mountain and showed him all the kingdoms of the world and their splendor.

"All this I will give you," he said, "if you will bow down and worship me."

Jesus said to him, "Away from me, Satan! For it is written: 'Worship the Lord your God, and serve him only.'"

Then the devil left him, and angels came and attended him.

Matthew 4:1-11 NIV

The Battle Is Over Our Future

Jesus was led by the Spirit into the wilderness, and He came out of the wilderness in the power of the Spirit. If Satan attacked Jesus, you can be sure he will attack you. Moses began his ministry at eighty, but Pharaoh attacked him before he was two. We need to understand that the battle is over our future.

Satan attacked Jesus in the area of His greatest need. What was it? Jesus had prayed and fasted for forty days. He was hungry. Satan told Jesus to turn stones into bread. Satan tempted Jesus right before He was about to enter into God's plans for His life — the ministry. Satan tempted Jesus to doubt Who He was when he said, "*If you be the Son of God.*" Jesus didn't joke with the devil. He didn't dialogue with the devil. He spoke the Word of God. He said, "It is written...It is written...It is written...." His retorts to the devil were three verses from Deuteronomy: 8:3, 6:16, and 6:13.

He Faced It as a Man

Jesus allowed Himself to be tempted in all areas of His body, soul, and spirit. He willingly suffered through that forty-day fast and faced temptation as a man, not as God, so He could sympathize with our weaknesses and show us we can overcome temptation as well. He did it for our sakes, not His own.

For we do not have a High Priest who cannot sympathize with our weaknesses, but was in all points tempted as we are, yet without sin.

Let us therefore come boldly to the throne of grace, that we may obtain mercy and find grace to help in time of need.

Hebrews 4:15,16 NKJV

Jesus is our pattern of total submission and humility. What areas of your life need to be submitted to the Lord and to others in authority over you? Look at the areas in your life where you experience the greatest trials. Examine your attitudes and action — or lack of action — in how you are handling these trials or have handled them in the past. Search for any cracks in your spiritual armor, such as unforgiveness, bitterness, lust, hurtful words spoken, pride, etc. Seek the wise counsel of a family member, friend, or pastor, and do an honest checkup of your physical, emotional, and spiritual walk. Don't hold back or let fear stop you from humbling yourself before the Lord and those God has put in authority over you. And remember, you're not in it alone.

Humble yourselves, therefore, under God's mighty hand, that he may lift you up in due time.

Cast all your anxiety on him because he cares for you.

Be self-controlled and alert. Your enemy the devil prowls around like a roaring lion looking for someone to devour.

Resist him, standing firm in the faith, because you know that your brothers throughout the world are undergoing the same kind of sufferings.

1 Peter 5:6-9 NIV

Prepare for Battle

Jesus prepared Himself for battle before He met Satan. Jesus knew Who He was, and He knew His enemy. Jesus chose His weapons and battleground carefully. He spoke boldly with authority, stood His ground, and didn't waver or give up even when the enemy kept coming back.

Let's explore the principles Jesus demonstrated for us. How did He prepare for battle? He was baptized of the water and the Spirit. Jesus knew His time was come to fulfill His Father's purpose. In obedience and under submission to His Father, Jesus' baptism by water symbolizes His death and resurrection, the cleansing of sins by the washing of the water.

We need to be water baptized to symbolize our willingness to die to self and our acceptance of Jesus as Lord in our lives. As we enter the water, our sin nature is washed clean (put under the blood of Jesus), and we rise up out of the water into new resurrected life in Christ. For us, baptism is an act of submission and obedience. It is a message to Satan that tells him loud and clear, "I'm one of God's kids, so don't mess with me!"

> *Jesus answered, "Most assuredly, I say to you, unless one is born of water and the Spirit, he cannot enter the kingdom of God."*
>
> John 3:5 NKJV

Yoke-Destroying, Burden-Removing Power

Jesus' baptism by the Spirit was an outpouring of the anointing of the Holy Spirit which provided Him with the yoke-destroying, burden-removing power of God to do all He was called to do in His ministry. We don't read of any miracles performed by Jesus until after He was baptized. This was the beginning of His three and one-half years of ministry prior to His death and resurrection. John the Baptist testified that Jesus was indeed the Lamb of God come to take away the sins of the world and that He would baptize us with the Holy Spirit.

*The next day John saw Jesus coming toward him,
and said, "Behold! The Lamb of God who takes
away the sin of the world!"*

John 1:29 NKJV

*And John bore witness, saying, "I saw the Spirit
descending from heaven like a dove, and He remained
upon Him.*

*"I did not know Him, but He who sent me to
baptize with water said to me, 'Upon whom you see
the Spirit descending, and remaining on Him, this is
He who baptizes with the Holy Spirit.'*

*"And I have seen and testified that this is the Son
of God."*

John 1:32-34 NKJV

We also need the anointing of the Holy Spirit to give
us the power to fulfill the great commission Jesus spoke of
just before He ascended to heaven. He "commanded" His
disciples to wait in Jerusalem to receive this baptism He
had promised.

*And being assembled together with them, He
commanded them not to depart from Jerusalem, but
to wait for the Promise of the Father, "which," He
said, "you have heard from Me;*

> "For John truly baptized with water, but you
> shall be baptized with the Holy Spirit not many days
> from now."
>
> Acts 1:4,5 NKJV

> But you shall receive power when the Holy Spirit
> has come upon you; and you shall be witnesses to Me
> in Jerusalem, and in all Judea and Samaria, and to
> the end of the earth.
>
> Acts 1:8 NKJV

That anointing and the gifts of the Holy Spirit are just as important for us today as they were for the disciples. Jesus knew we would have need of a Helper in order to fulfill our destiny and calling.

> Now He who establishes us with you in Christ
> and has anointed us is God,
> Who also has sealed us and given us the Spirit in
> our hearts as a deposit.
>
> 2 Corinthians 1:21,22 NKJV

> And I will pray the Father, and He will give you
> another Helper, that He may abide with you forever —
> The Spirit of truth, whom the world cannot
> receive, because it neither sees Him nor knows Him;

*but you know Him, for He dwells with you and will
be in you.*

John 14:16,17 NKJV

Another way Jesus prepared for His ministry and to
meet the devil in His time of tempting was fasting and
prayer. He fasted for forty days and forty nights. Fasting is
an act of humility that crucifies the flesh in us. Isaiah
speaks of the type of fast that pleases God.

*Is this not the fast that I have chosen: to loose the
bonds of wickedness, to undo the heavy burdens, to let
the oppressed go free, and that you break every yoke?*

*Then your light shall break forth like the
morning, your healing shall spring forth speedily, and
your righteousness shall go before you; the glory of the
Lord shall be your rear guard.*

*Then you shall call, and the Lord will answer;
you shall cry, and He will say, "Here I am."*

Isaiah 58:6,8,9 NKJV

Denying the Flesh

When faced with trials and troubles, what better way
to prepare to meet the Lord and to hear His voice than to
humble yourself with a fast? This does not mean you have
to fast for forty days. Just seek the Lord and let Him show

you how to fast and for how long. It might just be one meal, or it might be for a period of time to fast from specific foods (such as sweets) or from distractions that keep you from spending time with Him (such as television or movies). The important point is your commitment to submit and deny your flesh so that you will be more sensitive to hear what the Spirit is saying to you.

Set aside a special time to pray and to read the Word during the time of your fast. And be sure to write out a specific list of what you are asking God to do. This helps you focus and gives you a great way to remember what He has done for you through the fast.

If you are seeking answers from the Lord or a breakthrough in your circumstances, fasting and prayer may be what is needed to get the enemy off your back! After all, God's Word says that goodness and mercy will follow you all your life. (See Psalm 23:6.) And don't forget to thank Him and give Him the praise when you get your breakthrough!

Know the Enemy

To be successful in winning battles, military generals agree it is critical to know the enemy. Jesus knew His enemy. Here's what we can learn about Satan from Jesus' experience in the wilderness: Satan knows the Word and can quote it verbatim. He is the tempter and will always appeal to our flesh first. He doesn't give up easily and comes back again and again. He is bold and full of pride. He is such a deceiver he has even deceived himself into thinking he is greater than God. He only responds to the Word of God not to our words.

Jesus knew Who He was in the Father and where His authority rested. He wasn't intimidated by the devil, and we don't need to be either. Here are just a few scriptures that reveal this.

I have come as a light into the world, that whoever believes in Me should not abide in darkness.

John 12:46 NKJV

I am the way, the truth, and the life. No one comes to the Father except through Me.

John 14:6 NKJV

For I have not spoken on My own authority; but the Father who sent Me gave Me a command, what I should say and what I should speak.

And I know that His command is everlasting life. Therefore, whatever I speak, just as the Father has told Me, so I speak.

John 12:49,50 NKJV

Which He worked in Christ when He raised Him
from the dead and seated Him at His right hand in the
heavenly places,

Far above all principality and power and might
and dominion, and every name that is named, not
only in this age but also in that which is to come.

And He put all things under His feet, and gave
Him to be head over all things to the church,

Which is His body, the fullness of Him who fills
all in all.

Ephesians 1:20-23 NKJV

Just as Jesus knew Who He was in the Father and where His authority rested, we must know who we are in Christ and what authority we have been given.

As I began my speaking career, I watched other speakers. I wanted to be one of the best, so I made it a point to watch the best. I'd go over to the Billy Graham museum that's in our town. They've got a beautiful film there on the life of Billy Graham narrated by Paul Harvey. I watched that film so many times I started to hold my Bible like Billy Graham. Pretty soon I was pointing my finger like Billy Graham. After a while I started talking like Billy Graham, "And may the Lord bless you real good." And I'd practice my Billy Graham gestures and pose. But you know what, I found out when you imitate somebody else, nobody's there inside you.

See, you're an original. There's only one of you — born an original, don't die a copy — born a champion, don't die a loser. God's got a plan for you. Your plan may not be the plan He gave Billy Graham. It may not be the one He gave to Dr. James Dobson. It may not be the one for Mary Kay Ash, but God has got a plan. You're an original in God, and there's never ever been anybody like you. You're somebody in God.

> *"For I know the plans I have for you," declares the Lord, "plans to prosper you and not to harm you, plans to give you hope and a future."*
>
> *Jeremiah 29:11 NIV*

Your Authority in Jesus

Do you know who that somebody is? When you really get a grasp of who you are IN CHRIST and what your authority is, you will truly walk in victory over the enemy. *The Amplified Bible* says it best in these Scriptures.

> *Behold! I have given you authority and power to trample upon serpents and scorpions, and [physical and mental strength and ability] over all the power*

that the enemy [possesses]; and nothing shall in any
way harm you.

Luke 10:19 AMP

Little children, you are of God [you belong to
Him] and have [already] defeated and overcome them
[the agents of the antichrist], because He Who lives in
you is greater (mightier) that he who is in the world.

1 John 4:4 AMP

How much clearer can it get! Jesus has delegated His
authority to us. We are His Body — His Church. The
source of our authority is found in the resurrection and
exalting of Christ by God the Father. The only way we can
get a grasp of this is by spiritual revelation. It is more than
our natural minds can comprehend. So pray Ephesians
1:17-19 over yourself and personalize it as follows:

"May the God of my Lord Jesus Christ, the
Father of glory, give to me the spirit of wisdom
and revelation in the knowledge of Him,
"The eyes of my understanding being
enlightened; that I may know what is the hope of
His calling, what are the riches of the glory of His
inheritance in me and all the saints,

"And what is the exceeding greatness of His power toward us who believe, according to His mighty power."

We have the authority, but we must believe in that authority by faith. When we resist the enemy, we don't always see an immediate manifestation or change in our circumstances. If you keep your eyes on circumstances and base your faith on outward, natural manifestations, you can become discouraged easily. That is the tactic of the enemy. You must base your faith on the Word and believe it in your heart. Keep the battle in the spiritual realm. Smith Wigglesworth often said, "I'm not moved by what I see. I'm not moved by what I feel, I'm moved only by what I believe."[1]

What is faith? It is the confident assurance that something we want is going to happen. It is the certainty that what we hope for is waiting for us, even though we cannot see it up ahead.

Hebrews 11:1 TLB

Not only do we have the authority, but we also have the responsibility to exercise that authority. Since Jesus has delegated His authority to the Church (the Body of Christ) and we are part of the Body, then we are responsible for acting on that authority. God is not going to do it for us. The members of the Church (the Body) are God's hands and feet on this earth. That means, if the enemy is beating up on us, it's our own fault. That's just plain telling it like it is! God's done all He's going to do. We have the authority, so we must believe it, act on it, and stand our ground!

Choose Your Weapons

Going back to Jesus' temptation in the wilderness, we see that He chose His weapons and battleground carefully. He knew what it would take to resist the devil. He was alert and listened to what Satan said, and then He spoke the pure Word clearly and with authority. He didn't engage in any other conversation with Satan, and He didn't argue with him or get in the flesh. By doing this, He maintained control of the battleground in the spiritual realm and didn't allow any diversionary tactics to catch Him off balance.

Satan must respond to the Word of God, but he doesn't have to listen to our words, whining, or arguments. Remember, the weapons of our warfare are not carnal, because we don't wrestle against flesh and blood. (See Ephesians 6:12.) Don't let the enemy trick you into fighting in the flesh. You must fight with your spiritual weapons in order to win.

For the word of God is living and powerful, and sharper than any two-edged sword, piercing even to the division of soul and spirit, and of joints and morrow, and is a discerner of the thoughts and intents of the heart.

Hebrews 4:12 NKJV

Thank God, He gave us such powerful weapons — the Word and the Holy Spirit. He gave us weapons, but it is up to us to use them. We must get the foundation of the Word hidden in our hearts so that when the enemy comes, we can speak it out boldly and with authority.

When Jesus was standing on top of the temple in the Holy City, He didn't have time to go find His Bible and look up the right scriptures to come back at Satan. You're not going to have time either, so settle it in your heart that you must spend time in the Word and get it not just into your head, but into your heart.

King David said this so beautifully in Psalm 119. It is one of the longest psalms, yet one of the most powerful. Get your Bible and take a highlighter and search out the verses in that psalm that speak to you. Pray and ask the Lord to give you a heart like David.

Here are just a few lines from Psalm 119 NKJV that I meditate on and pray over and over, "Your Word I have hidden in my heart, that I might not sin against You....

Strengthen me according to Your word.... I will run the course of Your commandments, for You shall enlarge my heart...Incline my heart to Your testimonies.... Your word is a lamp to my feet and a light to my path.... You are my hiding place and my shield; I hope in Your word."

You can do the same thing with other scriptures. When you turn them into personal prayers, they become especially meaningful and sink into your heart. Pray and ask the Holy Spirit to enlighten you and give you discernment of the scriptures you need for specific situations. When you don't know what to do, or when you need help discerning a situation, depend on the Holy Spirit to guide you and help you and to bring the right scriptures to your remembrance. You may not have time to go find your Bible, but you do have time to quietly ask the Holy Spirit to give you the right words to speak.

But the Helper, the Holy Spirit, whom the Father will send in My name, He will teach you all things, and bring to your remembrance all things that I said to you.

John 14:26 NKJV

However, when He, the Spirit of truth, has come, He will guide you into all truth; for He will not speak on His own authority, but whatever He hears

He will speak; and He will tell you things to come.

He will glorify Me, for He will take of what is Mine and declare it to you.

John 16:13,14 NKJV

Okay, so now we have prepared ourselves to meet the enemy. We know who we are in Christ. We've chosen our weapons and the battleground. We know we have authority delegated to us by Jesus, and we've accepted our responsibility to put it to use.

You're thinking, *I'm still getting attacked. The circumstances haven't gotten any better. What's left to do?* Jesus stood His ground and didn't waver, and that's what you have to do too. Satan doesn't give up easily. He keeps coming back trying to wear you down. So stand boldly on the Word in faith and walk in love. Keep pressing in. Don't give up!

Meditate on these scriptures:

Be on your guard; stand firm in the faith, be men (and women) of courage; be strong.

Do everything in love.

1 Corinthians 16:13,14 NIV

It is for freedom that Christ has set us free. Stand firm, then, and do not let yourselves be burdened again by a yoke of slavery.

Galatians 5:1 NIV

I have been crucified with Christ; it is no longer I who live, but Christ lives in me; and the life which I now live in the flesh I live by faith in the Son of God, who loved me and gave Himself for me.

Galatians 2:20 NKJV

Therefore you are no longer a slave but a son, and if a son, then an heir of God through Christ.

Galatians 4:7 NKJV

Your attitude should be the same as that of Christ Jesus:

Who, being in very nature God, did not consider equality with God something to be grasped,

but made himself nothing, taking the very nature of a servant, being made in human likeness.

And being found in appearance as a man, he humbled himself and became obedient to death — even death on a cross!

Therefore God exalted him to the highest place and gave him the name that is above every name.

Philippians 2:5-9 NIV

...But one thing I do, forgetting those things which are behind and reaching forward to those things which are ahead,

I press toward the goal for the prize of the upward call of God in Christ Jesus.

Philippians 3:13,14 NKJV

Finally, my brethren, be strong in the Lord, and in the power of his might.

Ephesians 6:10

For we are made partakers of Christ, if we hold the beginning of our confidence stedfast to the end.

Hebrews 3:14

Let us hold fast the profession of our faith without wavering; (for he is faithful that promised.)

Hebrews 10:23

But when they deliver you up, do not worry about how or what you should speak. For it will be given to you in that hour what you should speak;

> *For it is not you who speak, but the Spirit of your*
> *Father who speaks in you.*
> Matthew 10:19,20 NKJV

Q: When have you found it wise to flee from temptation?

Q: What areas of your life will you submit to the Lord today?

Q: How do you plan to use your weapons more effectively in the future?

Chapter 7

DEVELOP A PRAISE MENTALITY

*I will bless the Lord at all times: his praise shall
continually be in my mouth.*

Psalm 34:1

Have you ever spent time with people who live Psalm
34? All you hear is, "Hallelujah! Glory to God! Thank
You, Jesus! Praise the Lord!" coming out of their mouths
constantly, when you know for a fact they're facing a
multitude of problems. That's a praise mentality. That's
not parroting. That's proof that out of the abundance of
the heart, the mouth speaks. They have a praise mentality.

Now I know what you're thinking. *I just don't know
how they can be so happy all the time when the devil is
knocking on their door with troubles worse than I've ever seen.
I admire them, but that's just not me.* Well friend, if you're
thinking that, you've been listening to the devil whisper
in your ear too long, saying things like, "You don't want
to look foolish.... All those words sound so phony.... Just
look at your circumstances.... What would people
think?... They'll call you a religious fanatic if you start
talking that way all the time." Sound familiar?

If you've really decided to take back what the enemy
has stolen from you, if you have set your face like flint to

resist the devil and want to see him flee, then start building a praise mentality into your life today. Now you're saying, "Okay, but I'm not musical. I can't carry a tune in a bucket. And besides that, I'm in the worst storm of my life and I'm tired."

The Devil Hates That Kind of Shoutin'

Praise isn't just music, although God delights in our praise whether we can sing in tune or not. Sing or speak the Word of God over your circumstances continuously. Praise God with your mouth for Who He is and who you are in Him. Thank Him for His promises every chance you get.

Don't wait for things to get better. Start doing it before they get better so they do get better. You can shout it out, and I guarantee the devil won't stay around long. He hates that kind of shoutin', and he especially hates praise that is focused on God and not himself.

David was one of the greatest praisers ever to walk this earth. The Psalms he wrote are beautiful to read or to sing, but more than that, they are powerful in defeating the enemy. We need to follow David's example and study what he did and how God responded.

Time after time we see how David sang praises to the Lord and openly and shamelessly worshipped Him in the midst of the most difficult circumstances. He danced with abandonment before the Lord, played instruments, and sang praises. What an encouragement the Psalms are today, thousands of years after they were written. If you're feeling discouraged, just go to the Psalms, and you won't be able to stay that way long.

When David wrote Psalm 34, he was in grave danger. King Saul was seeking to kill him. Running for his life, David was brought before King Abimelech in the land of the Philistines. When he discovered that the Philistines knew who he was, David was afraid and pretended to be insane in order to escape. Even though he was in perilous circumstances, we see David's heart was tender before the Lord. He didn't blame God. He made a quality decision that he would praise the Lord "at all times," no matter what happened, and his praises would be "continuous." He "boasted in the Lord" and "rejoiced."

The Power of Corporate Praise

David also knew the power of corporate praise and encouraged others to join with him. We see this in Psalm 34:3, which has become so familiar to us in a modern praise song: "O magnify the Lord with me, and let us exalt his name together."

Then came the deliverance. David wrote in verse four, "I sought the Lord, and he heard me, and delivered me from all my fears." Wow, is that powerful or what? Why can't we grasp how simple it is?

Verse five explains why those people we know who are constantly praising the Lord in the midst of their

troubles have such joy and brightness in their counte-
nances: "They looked unto him, and were lightened: and
their faces were not ashamed" (Psalm 34:5). How much
better we feel when we are smiling than when we are
scowling and down in the dumps.

The Weapon of Praise

I hope you have guessed by now that praise is actually
another weapon God has put in our quiver of arrows.
When we learn to use it continuously, the enemy can't rob
us of our joy, which the Lord says is our strength.

> *Do not sorrow, for the joy of the Lord is your*
> *strength.*
>
> *Nehemiah 8:10 NKJV*

Praise and the use of musical instruments were an
important part in the battle plans of the armies of Israel.
At Jericho, the priests blew trumpets as they walked
around the walled city.

> *So the people shouted when the priests blew with*
> *the trumpets: and it came to pass, when the people*
> *heard the sound of the trumpet, and the people shouted*
> *with a great shout, that the wall fell down flat.*
>
> *Joshua 6:20*

Praise and worship was an important part of the preparation for battle. King Jehoshaphat, a descendent of King David, followed after the ways of David and was a worshipper of the Lord. When the armies of Moab and Ammon declared war against Judah, King Jehoshaphat sought the Lord and proclaimed a fast throughout the land of Judah.

People from all the cities came together seeking the Lord. They humbled themselves before the Lord and prayed, speaking His promises and His goodness. They submitted what seemed an impossible situation to the Lord, admitting they could not do anything of themselves and keeping their eyes on Him. The Lord spoke to them through a prophet and told them not to be afraid, that the battle was not theirs but the Lord's, and they would not have to fight in this battle. They believed, worshipped God, and were obedient.

And Jehoshaphat bowed his head with his face to the ground: and all Judah and the inhabitants of Jerusalem fell before the Lord, worshipping the Lord.

And the Levites...stood up to praise the Lord God of Israel with a loud voice on high.

2 Chronicles 20:18,19

And Jehoshaphat sent out the praisers and musicians in front of the warriors. They stood and watched the miraculous hand of the Lord deliver them from their enemies without lifting one weapon in their hands. The weapon they used was praise.

> *He appointed singers unto the Lord, and that should praise the beauty of holiness, as they went out before the army, and to say, Praise the Lord; for his mercy endureth for ever.*
>
> *And when they began to sing and to praise, the Lord set ambushments against the children of Ammon, Moab, and mount Seir, which were come against Judah; and they were smitten.*
>
> *2 Chronicles 20:21,22*

Songs of Deliverance

The Scriptures also document how great men and women of Israel sang songs of deliverance and praised the Lord. These songs were often quite lengthy and told the story of all the Lord did for them. They gave the Lord all the glory. Let's look at a couple of them.

After Moses and the children of Israel crossed the Red Sea, they sang a glorious song unto the Lord. And then Miriam took a tambourine and led the women in dances and song.

Then sang Moses and the children of Israel this song unto the Lord, and spake, saying, I will sing unto the Lord, for he hath triumphed gloriously: the horse and his rider hath he thrown into the sea.

The Lord is my strength and song, and he is become my salvation: he is my God, and I will prepare him an habitation; my father's God, and I will exalt him.

The Lord is a man of war: the Lord is his name.

Exodus 15:1-3

And Miriam the prophetess, the sister of Aaron, took a timbrel in her hand; and all the women went out after her with timbrels and with dances.

Exodus 15:20

The children of Israel saw the Lord do great and mighty miracles and deliver them from vicious armies, and yet they were tempted and fell into sin and rebellion. God allowed them to be conquered many times because of their disobedience. But there were always a few strong and faithful ones who led the people back to God. Deborah, a prophetess and a judge, was one of these. She even went to battle and directed Barak, the son of Abinoam, as the Lord spoke through her. Together, Deborah and Barak won a miraculous victory and then sang a song of praise to the Lord. Here are just a few verses:

> Then sang Deborah and Barak the son of Abinoam on that day, saying,
> Praise ye the Lord for the avenging of Israel, when the people willingly offered themselves.
> Hear, O ye kings; give ear, O ye princes; I, even I, will sing unto the Lord; I will sing praise to the Lord God of Israel.
>
> Judges 5:1-3

We see examples of the power of praise in the New Testament as well. I like the story Jack Hayford tells about two men who had no reason to be shouting about anything — Paul and Silas. We know they weren't the Frozen Chosen, because they were in jail. If they were the First Church of the Frigidaire, they probably would have been holding a meeting on prison reform. We know they weren't the Assembly of Whiners and Complainers, or they'd have been having a pity party because the pastor hadn't been by to see them. They must have been from one of those Christian Praise Gatherings, because they were singing and shouting at midnight.

They were thanking God, and they had no reason to thank God, sitting there in a jail — blacker than a thousand midnights, cold, damp, stinking. Paul's back had been beaten right down to the very bone, not with spaghetti but with leather strips tied off on the ends with sharp metal that ripped his skin open.

Sitting there in the back of that cell, chained to the wall, Paul said, "Hey, Silas."

Silas said, "Paul, what is it?"

"I feel a hallelujah coming on."

"You mean right here?"

"I mean, right here in this jail."

Silas said, "Well, you go ahead. You lead out, and I'll join in with you."

And they began — in that cold, dark, damp cell with the rats running between their feet — to praise and shout to the living God.

Remember what happened? An earthquake shook the jail, the doors were opened, and their chains fell off. (See Acts 16:19-26.) Now that's the kind of results we all want to have. It all began with singing and shouting praises to the Lord in the midst of the worst of circumstances. So, don't ever let anyone tell you there isn't power in praise.

The key to a breakthrough in the spiritual realm is when you decide to decide — without a praise and worship team, without a whole slew of music cassettes — to become a worshipper of God. I tell you, that cell filled up with praise. It filtered through the bars and floated right out through the windows and up into the atmosphere. They kept praising and shouting to God 'til it got into the stratosphere. They kept on praising and shouting to God 'til it got up into the ionosphere and flowed right on up into the very throne room of God.

God said, "I hear a song." The angels said, "Well, of course You do. This is heaven. Everybody's singing up here." God said, "No, this is a song of two men in trouble. Listen to that beat. I hear a song. Listen to that music that's flowing up this way. That's the sound of a man in trouble. That's the sound of a man praising Me when there's no reason to praise. He's hoping when there's nothing to hope in except his relationship with Me. He's worshipping Me."

God began to get happy. The angels got happy. There was dancing and rejoicing in heaven. God said, "Glory to Myself...Hallelujah. I mean, I hear a song."

The Bible says heaven is God's throne; earth is His footstool. And God got up and began to tap His feet; and when God tapped His feet, it shook planet earth, and the doors of that jail flew open, and Paul and Silas were set free and the jailer and his entire household got saved.

I tell you, buy all the tapes and books you want, but while you're doing it, you better be shouting the praises of the living God. Because God watches over His Word and hastens to perform it, and He will perform it in your life.

A Ladder of Praise

Merlin Carothers describes a vision of a ladder of praise in his book, *Prison to Praise*. This vision so clearly explains the victory available to us if we continue to praise the Lord through the toughest circumstances, that I want to share it with you in its entirety. Here's what he saw:

I saw a beautiful, bright summer day. The air was filled with light, and I had a sense of everything being beautiful. Up above was a heavy, solid black cloud beyond which nothing could be seen. A ladder extended from the ground up into the black cloud. At the base of the ladder were hundreds of people trying to get a chance at climbing the ladder. They had heard that above the blackness there was something more beautiful than anything a human eye had ever seen, something that brought unbelievable joy to those who reached it. As person after person tried to ascend they quickly climbed to the lower edge of the clouds. The crowd watched to see what would happen.

In a short while the person would come wildly sliding down the ladder and fall into the crowd scattering people in all directions. They reported that once they got into the blackness they lost all sense of direction.

My time finally came, and as I made my way up the ladder into the blackness, it grew so intense that I could feel its power nearly forcing me to give up and slide back. But step by step I continued upward until suddenly my eyes beheld the most intense brightness I had ever seen. It was a brilliant whiteness too glorious to describe in words. As I came out above the dark cloud, I realized that I could walk on top of it. As I looked into the brightness, I was able to walk without difficulty. When I looked down to examine the nature of the cloud, I immediately began to sink. Only by looking at the brightness could I stay on top.

Then the scene changed and I was back looking at all three levels from a distance. "What does it all mean?" I asked, and the answer came:

"The brightest sunshine below the cloud is the light that many Christians live in and accept as normal. The ladder is the ladder of praising Me. Many try to climb and learn to praise Me in all things. At first they are very eager, but when they get into things that they don't understand they become confused and cannot hold on. They lose faith and go sliding back. As they fall, they injure other people who have been hoping to find a way to live in continual joy and praise.

"Those who make it through those difficult times reach a new world and realize that the life they once thought of as normal cannot be compared to the life I have prepared for those who praise Me and believe that I carefully watch over them. He who reaches the light of the heavenly kingdom can walk on top of difficulties no matter how dark they may seem as long as he keeps his eyes off the problem and on My victory in Christ. No matter how difficult it may seem to trust Me to work in every detail in your life, keep clinging to the ladder of praise and move upwards!"[1]

Most of us truly underestimate the power of praise. God does inhabit the praise of His people, and when we praise Him, all heaven joins us. Learn how to use this weapon. Remember, Satan was the praise and worship leader in heaven, and he hates to hear us worshipping God instead of him. Satan flees when we praise the living God.

So start praising and don't give up, no matter what the circumstances or how bad you feel. Keep your eyes on Jesus and climb right on up above the clouds. Keep climbing on up into the throne room. Satan can't follow you there. Don't let the enemy or the cares of the day distract you and cause you to slide back down the ladder.

Sing and shout and dance your way to victory. You're a part of a chosen generation, a royal priesthood, a child of the King. You were created to praise Him and to let others see how He has called you out of darkness into the marvelous light. You have unlimited access to the King of kings, and He welcomes you into His courts of praise. Go there often. Let His light shine in you so others will want what you have.

Meditate on these scriptures:

> *But you are a chosen people, a royal priesthood, a holy nation, a people belonging to God, that you may declare the praises of him who called you out of darkness into his wonderful light.*
>
> *1 Peter 2:9 NIV*

> *Know ye that the Lord he is God: it is he that hath made us, and not we ourselves; we are his people, and the sheep of his pasture.*
>
> *Enter into his gates with thanksgiving, and into his courts with praise: be thankful unto him, and bless his name.*
>
> *Psalm 100:3,4*

> *But let all those that put their trust in thee rejoice: let them ever shout for joy, because thou*

defendest them: let them also that love thy name be joyful in thee.

Psalm 5:11

O Lord, our Lord, how majestic is your name in all the earth! You have set your glory above the heavens.

From the lips of children and infants you have ordained praise because of your enemies, to silence the foe and the avenger.

Psalm 8:1,2 NIV

I will praise thee, O Lord, with my whole heart; I will shew forth all thy marvellous works.

I will be glad and rejoice in thee: I will sing praise to thy name, O thou most High.

When mine enemies are turned back, they shall fall and perish at thy presence.

Psalm 9:1-3

Thou wilt shew me the path of life: in thy presence is fulness of joy; at thy right hand there are pleasures for evermore.

Psalm 16:11

I will call upon the Lord, who is worthy to be praised: so shall I be saved from mine enemies.

Psalm 18:3

The Lord liveth; and blessed be my rock; and let the God of my salvation be exalted.

It is God that avengeth me, and subdueth the people under me.

He delivereth me from mine enemies.

Psalm 18:46-48

The Lord is my light and my salvation; whom shall I fear? the Lord is the strength of my life; of whom shall I be afraid?

Psalm 27:1

The Lord is my strength and my shield; my heart trusted in him, and I am helped: therefore my heart greatly rejoiceth; and with my song will I praise him.

Psalm 28:7

Thou art my hiding place; thou shalt preserve me from trouble; thou shalt compass me about with songs of deliverance. Selah.

Psalm 32:7

Delight thyself also in the Lord; and he shall give thee the desires of thine heart.

Psalm 37:4

Yet the Lord will command his lovingkindness in the daytime, and in the night his song shall be with me, and my prayer unto the God of my life.

Psalm 42:8

The Lord's blessing is our greatest wealth. All our work adds nothing to it!

Proverbs 10:22 TLB

The name of the Lord is a strong tower: the righteous runneth into it, and is safe.

Proverbs 18:10

To appoint unto them...beauty for ashes, the oil of joy for mourning, the garment of praise for the spirit of heaviness; that they might be called trees of righteousness, the planting of the Lord, that he might be glorified.

For as the earth bringeth forth her bud, and as the garden causeth the things that are sown in it to spring forth; so the Lord God will cause righteousness and praise to spring forth before all the nations.

Isaiah 61:3,11

For ye shall go out with joy, and be led forth with peace; the mountains and the hills shall break forth before you into singing, and all the trees of the field shall clap their hands.

Isaiah 55:12

And they shall be my people and I will be their God.

And I will give them one heart and mind to worship me forever, for their own good and for the good of all their descendants.

And I will make an everlasting covenant with them, promising never again to desert them, but only to do them good. I will put a desire into their hearts to worship me, and they shall never leave me.

Jeremiah 32:38-40 TLB

Q: How have you used praise to battle the enemy in the past?

Q: How can you use it more effectively as a weapon?

Q: What will you do to incorporate more praise into your daily walk and talk?

Chapter 8

WAGE WAR ON THE DEVIL

And from the days of John the Baptist until now the kingdom of heaven suffereth violence, and the violent take it by force.

Matthew 11:12

In the previous chapters we explored all the important "to dos" for preparing to take back what's been stolen. By now I hope you've made a quality decision to take it all back, stopped blaming God for the trials and difficulties in your life, gotten honest before God, sought true repentance, done what's right to make amends and restitution, developed a new focus by zeroing in on solutions and discovering who you are IN CHRIST, submitted yourself to the Lord, learned how to resist the devil, and developed a praise mentality. Now it's time to get tough and wage war on the devil. That means it is time to go into battle and take back what is rightfully yours.

Did you know that God made 32,000 promises to us in the Bible? And do you know for whom Jesus purchased these promises with His blood on Calvary? He did it for His Church — the *ecclesia* — the "called-out ones."[1] Jesus has already done that for all of us who belong to Him. That means it's already ours. Wow!

Get that down in your heart and spirit — all things pertaining to life and godliness belong to you and Satan has no right to them. They are already yours. If you haven't claimed them as your own, it is time to rise up and take them!

> *According as his divine power hath given unto us all things that pertain unto life and godliness, through the knowledge of him that hath called us to glory and virtue:*
>
> *Whereby are given unto us exceeding great and precious promises: that by these ye might be partakers of the divine nature, having escaped the corruption that is in the world through lust.*
>
> *2 Peter 1:3,4*

Go Ahead and Roar Back

The devil may be walking around like a roaring lion, but you are a member of the tribe of Judah. Your Commander in Chief is the "Lion of Judah," the "Captain of the hosts of heaven." You're a joint heir seated on the right hand of the Father. You've been given *all* authority to war in His name. So go ahead and roar back at the enemy when he tries to kill, steal, or destroy you or anything God has given to you.

Don't take it any more. Put him on the run! He fears the power you have IN CHRIST! Always be ready. Put on your armor every single day, use your weapons violently if necessary, and when you have done all, stand — believing in the power He has given you!

> *Finally, my brethren, be strong in the Lord, and in the power of his might.*
>
> *Put on the whole armour of God, that ye may be able to stand against the wiles of the devil.*
>
> *For we wrestle not against flesh and blood, but against principalities, against powers, against the rulers of the darkness of this world, against spiritual wickedness in high places.*
>
> *Wherefore take unto you the whole armour of God, that ye may be able to withstand in the evil day, and having done all, to stand.*
>
> *Ephesians 6:10-13*

To wrestle with someone means to contend by grappling with and striving to throw an opponent off balance or to engage in as if in a violent or determined struggle.[2] To wrestle with someone, you must be in hand-to-hand combat. Now that's getting into the heat of the battle when it comes down to such close contact with an enemy.

To take something means to get into one's hands or into one's possession, power, or control; to get possession of by killing or capturing; to catch or attack through the effect of a sudden force or influence; to transfer to one's own keeping.[3] According to *Strong's Exhaustive Concordance*, "take" means to seize, pluck, pull, or take by force.[4]

Matthew Henry's Commentary on this chapter's foundational verse, Matthew 11:12, says we must show fervency and zeal, run, wrestle, be in an agony to win the prize, have such a strong desire for the great salvation that we must have it at all cost, show diligence and be in holy contention to enter the kingdom of heaven.[5] These are pretty strong words of action. Does that give you a better idea of how we are to wage this war against our enemy, the devil?

On the day Winston Churchill became prime minister of Great Britain at the beginning of World War II, an excerpt of his speech depicts what a war victory in the natural requires: "I have nothing to offer but blood, toil, tears, and sweat. You ask, what is our policy? I will say: It is to wage war by sea, land, and air, with all our might and with all the strength God can give us. That is our policy. You ask, what is our aim? I can answer in one word: It is victory. Victory at all costs. Victory in spite of all terror. Victory however long and hard the road may be; for without victory, there is no survival."[6]

Aim for Victory

How then should we approach war in the spiritual realm? With the same furor, the same violence, the same willingness to do battle no matter how long it takes to win, the same awareness that without victory there is no survival. But the difference is that Jesus has already won the victory for us.

We are here on this earth simply to enforce that victory. We do not need to fear the enemy, but we must respect him. Satan knows his time is short, and that makes him fight all the harder and more viciously. He hates us and wants to destroy (neutralize, render useless, annihilate) us.[7]

It is also important to remember nothing happens in the natural realm that doesn't first happen in the spiritual realm. That means war in the heavenlies is as violent, maybe even more so, as it is in the natural. We can read about such a battle in the Scriptures.

> Then he said, "Don't be frightened, Daniel, for your request has been heard in heaven and was answered the very first day you began to fast before the Lord and pray for understanding; that very day I was sent here to meet you.
>
> But for twenty-one days the mighty Evil Spirit who overrules the kingdom of Persia blocked my way.

> *Then Michael, one of the top officers of the heavenly*
> *army, came to help me, so that I was able to break*
> *through these spirit rulers of Persia.*
>
> *Daniel 10:12,13 TLB*

But we have weapons more powerful than any the devil has. The Word of God is more powerful than a two-edged sword, bringing down the kingdoms of Satan and the imaginations of man. We have seen the power of praise defeat a whole army. And the greatest weapon we have in our arsenal is the blood of Jesus.

You must believe in these weapons and use them. You must believe God's Word is true and it will work for you. It's your faith in Him that causes His power to operate effectively in your life. If you believe God, no power on earth (Satan's realm) can stop you.

> *Then I heard a loud voice saying in heaven,*
> *"Now salvation, and strength, and the kingdom of*
> *our God, and the power of His Christ have come, for*
> *the accuser of our brethren, who accused them before*
> *our God day and night, has been cast down.*
>
> *"And they overcame him by the blood of the*
> *Lamb and by the word of their testimony, and they*
> *did not love their lives to the death."*
>
> *Revelation 12:10,11 NKJV*

Get Proactive

Steven Covey has written an excellent book titled *Seven Habits of Highly Effective People*. It would be an enhancement to your library. It's a great book for business people, but the principles apply to all walks of life. He says the number one habit that highly effective people have is they are proactive.[8]

You say, "What do you mean?" You've got to make something happen. You can't just sit back and assimilate information. You've got to apply information. You've got to be a doer of the Word and not a hearer only so you'll be blessed in your deeds. You and I have to become proactive.

I can't help but think back to an October morning a year or so ago. It was 8:00 in the morning — well, maybe it was 8:20. The doorbell rang. We weren't expecting anyone, but I went down to see who was there.

I opened up the inside door before opening up the screen, and who's there? Two nicely attired ladies with some papers in their hands. I said, "Ladies, may I help you?" They said, "Are you a Jehovah's Witness?" I said, "No, didn't even see the accident!" They said, "No, no, no, no. See, we're Jehovah's Witnesses, and we've got these papers called *The Watchtower*, and we're out making some...."

"Ohhh," I said, "well, of course, I'm a Jehovah's witness. I try to witness for Jehovah wherever I go. If you're a homemaker, which is not a second-class occupation according to Proverbs 31, you can create heaven on earth for your family. If you're a banker, you can handle the unsearchable riches of Christ. If you're a plumber, you can dispense the rivers of Living Water. If you're a farmer, you can plant the Seed of the Word. If you're an insurance man, like I was when I got saved, you can represent the Eternal Life Insurance Company."[9]

They said, "Where's your home office?" I said, "Calvary. The premium has already been paid. The more you draw, the more you get. We've got a rate book. It's all fine print, but you don't have to worry about it. You can have the Holy Spirit let you know just what you need to know just when you need to know it. We cover you for life, health, peace, and daily needs. We've got flight insurance. If you're on a plane, and it goes down, you get to go up. We've got you covered."

You don't have to look like one of the Blues Brothers in an ill-fitting suit down at the town square harassing people with a ten-pound Bible and a Have-You-Been-Washed-in-the-Blood pin on one lapel and Jesus-Saves on the other. The Bible says to be ready to give an answer for the hope that's within you.

If you want victory, don't walk around looking like you've been baptized in vinegar, spent the night upside down in a post hole, and served as the cruise director on the Titanic. You've got to put a smile on your face and a spring in your step. Some Christians look so miserable, I say, "Why don't you tell people you're an atheist and help us in reverse. We don't need anymore bad PR." That's all God wants you to do. Be ready to give an answer for the hope that's within you.

Living in the Evangelicals' Mecca, Wheaton, Illinois, I've never had a call from a Presbyterian, a Lutheran, a Baptist, a Catholic, or a charismatic. Nobody's been by — but the Jehovah's Witnesses were out there.

I said, "Come on in, ladies. Let me find you something to drink, and let's have a little discussion about the blood of Jesus." They said, "Say what?" I said, "Come on in. Let's talk about the blood." And it was like they had choreographed it, two finely attired women moonwalked right off my front porch. But they're out there, and they're doing something — being proactive. What are you and I doing?

Here's a story that tells what it means to wage war on the enemy. Dr. Lester Sumrall was ministering in the jungles of South America. He was taken into one of the villages and introduced to the village witch doctor who began satanic, demonic, supernatural incantations and whirling around in front of Dr. Sumrall.

Dr. Sumrall didn't pull out his daily planner and say, "Now, it's obvious, sir, that you have unmet needs in your life. You've not been self-actualized. You have basic youth conflicts that would cause you to act like this, and if we can get you into one of our Lester Sumrall Evangelistic Association 12-step programs, you may be able to recover from these problems." Dr. Lester Sumrall didn't operate that way. He put one hand on one side of the man's head, one hand on the other side of his head, looked straight into the man's eyes, and said, "Come out of him in the name of Jesus Christ of Nazareth." And it was like that man had been hit with a .357 magnum. He fell as though dead at Dr. Sumrall's feet and then got up praising God.

Put That Bed Back

It's now 2:00 in the morning. Dr. Sumrall is awakened by the presence of evil in his room. His bed is in the middle of the room, shaking, and trembling. He sits up in his bed and looks, not with his natural eyes but his spiritual eyes, and sees Satan himself standing at the foot of the bed. He said, "Oh, it's you. I was trying to get some sleep." He said, "In the name of Jesus, go from me in Jesus' name!" Jehovah Shalom shows up, and the peace of God fills that room.

It's quiet, the bed quits shaking, but here's what separates the ladies from the girls and the men from the boys. Dr. Sumrall thought to himself, *Now wait a minute. When I went to bed tonight, my bed was against the wall. Now it's here in the middle of the room.* Then he said,

"Satan, in the name of Jesus Christ of Nazareth, get back in here. In the name of Jesus, put my bed back where it was." That bed began to shake and tremble and vibrate, slide across that wall, bang up against that wall, and Dr. Sumrall put his head back down on his pillow and slept like a baby the rest of the night.

It's early December 1992 at the Crouch house. Our stockings have been hung by the chimney with care. (We'd worn them for months, and they needed the air.) We had had an incredible breakthrough with my daughter. But no sooner had we had that breakthrough when old Slewfoot himself came along to try to steal the victory just like it says in Mark 4:15, "...Satan cometh immediately, and taketh away the word that was sown in their hearts."

I got a call from an uncle you and I have in common. His name is Sam, and Uncle Sam said, "We believe that you've miscounted your blessings." And you say, "Now, you were being attacked by the devil." In a sense, but I had not listened to my wife's counsel. We were having some difficulties with our accountant, who had lost some of our documentation and paperwork.

My wife had set me down and said, "Van, we've got this problem. These forms don't seem to be filled out correctly, some of the calculations may not be right, and the forms weren't sent in on time." By not being diligent and following through on my obligations, I opened the door for the problems that came my way. When we open a door, then the enemy has access to come in and have a heyday.

Uncle Sam sent me a form — maybe you've gotten one like it — and what it said in short was that Uncle Sam planned to go into joint tenancy with me on my property. He was going to be sharing the house with me. In addition, under Statute 6331 he said he had the right to seize wages, bank accounts, commissions, and other income. You say, "What did you do?" We decided to do what Steven Covey talked about in his book, what Jesus displayed in his life — to become proactive.

You're thinking, *Well, I bet you had to cut back on some things.* Yes, but we didn't cut back on our tithe. We didn't cut back our offensive giving. You say, "What's that?" Offerings — what we give into the work of God's kingdom over and above our tithe. We paid our tithes and then some. We gave our offerings. We began to target our seed for a fair and equitable outcome to the situation.

The first thing I had to do was repent to the Father for my lack of diligence and agree to make it right with Uncle Sam. Then we began to believe God for favor with the authorities so that the enemy could not steal from us. You know what I found out. There are some nice people who work at the Internal Revenue Service, and if you will keep your word, and your yes is yes, and your no is no, they'll work with you. They said, "In thirty days you must send us a certified check for $20,123." And they said, "In ten days, you must notify us by certified mail how you plan to pay that amount in thirty days."

I don't know about most of you, but $20,000 is a lot of money at the Crouch house. However, in the time of trouble, we know we can call on Jehovah Jireh. And that's exactly what we did. We kept paying our tithe. We kept speaking the Word, and in the long and the short of it, we were shown supernatural favor. The IRS allowed us an extension of time to pay off the amount owed, and they eliminated over $5,000 in penalties.

Paid in Full

In four and a half months, our obligation to the IRS was paid in full. We went into the realm of the Spirit, and we put our foot down and said, "Devil, in Jesus' name, we're going to do what is right. Our seed will produce, and you can't stop it because God's Word says He will return the seed to the sower. It's ours in the name of Jesus Christ of Nazareth." God was faithful to do what He said He would do.

Let me tell you how God paid off the last $5,000 to the IRS. I had no speaking engagements for the first three weeks of March. God has dealt with me not to promote myself. You know, "Come all, see what a great speaker I am. You ought to have me." God said, "Don't do that. You can book yourself or you can go where I book you. Where I send you will be better than where you send yourself."

I had a four-day meeting with a wonderful Assembly of God men's camp in Hawaii. They said they would provide a discounted air ticket, and they would pay an honorarium. Now it hasn't taken long in ministry to know that means different things for different groups. In fact, at one church they said, "Don't discuss your honorarium." I said, "I won't. I'm as embarrassed about it as you are."

So I went to Hawaii for four days and stayed for three weeks. After the men's camp, the Lord multiplied my speaking engagements, and I stayed in a $12 million mansion built by the Japanese on Diamondhead resort for two and a half weeks. Arriving in Hawaii with a need for $5,000, God sent me home with twice as much. It didn't cost a dime to be there, and He paid off the last of the IRS while I spoke in Hawaii almost every day for three weeks.

I went to places that looked like they were going to pay me in pineapples and chickens, and a lot of the people showed up barefoot with flower leis around their necks. But in your lack, God will do exceedingly abundantly above all that you can ask or you can think.

God's System Is Best

God's got the best system. God will bring the victory when you need it. If you need a breakthrough today, if you're under a lot of pressure, let me encourage you to put the pressure on the Word of God. If you want more "fruitage" in your life, then you've got to have more "rootage." The only place to get that "rootage" is from the Word.

Mike Murdock says, "When you want something you've never had, you got to do something you've never done." Ask the Lord to show you what you need to do, to give you a battle plan. It may seem like the most foolish, ridiculous, out-to-lunch, goofball way to do things, but when God says do it, do it. He always makes a way for us even when all we see is a wilderness. Sometimes those wilderness experiences provide the greatest blessings. They are faith builders that take us to a higher level in Him.

The Seed of the Righteous

Earlier in the chapter I mentioned a breakthrough we had with my daughter. I want to share with you a testimony of how faithful God is if we don't give up. I had no idea prior to my marriage to Doni what challenges were in store for our blended family. I totally underestimated the great needs of my own children, Wendy and Brent, and how much restoration God was going to have to do. It wasn't long before our family learned that if we were in fact to see any victory in their lives, we would have to go to war and take back the ground the devil had stolen from our children, from me as a father, and from Doni as a mother.

In 1992 Doni and I decided to participate in Pastor Rod Parsley's World Harvest Resurrection Seed Offering. It's one offering, one hour. There are no pledges. The only figure that counts is cash in the bank at the close of business on Monday following that Sunday's service. On Easter Sunday we sowed a significant seed in that offering for my daughter.

Some people might have believed that we received a miraculous turnaround, but not unlike the woman with the issue of blood in Mark 5, my daughter was none better but rather grew worse. The heat of the battle intensified. She had four serious driving violations. She was living a life of rebellion against God and in rebellion to me as her father — a life that she would probably say was out of control.

It was Thanksgiving 1992, and we were at a World Harvest Camp Meeting in Columbus, Ohio. I was at the Holiday Inn up on the tenth floor under a heavy anointing for a nap. I had made a decision to go to Bedside Baptist with Pastor Pillow and Brother Sheets, laying there checking my eyelids for holes when the phone rang. It was my daughter, who reported that she was in Eagle River, Wisconsin.

My daughter had gone on a Thanksgiving trip with the man she thought was going to be her fiancé. However, he announced on that trip to his parents' home that he didn't really care anything about her and didn't want anything more to do with her. The parents indicated that if their son was to get married, Wendy was of the wrong faith — not that any of them were practicing any faith.

Wendy was stranded six hours north of Chicago. She had gone to a motel with her springer spaniel dog and cat while waiting for help to arrive. A couple who, interestingly enough, were on an anniversary getaway weekend, dropped everything they were doing, drove to Eagle River, Wisconsin, and brought my daughter to Chicago.

The following day we were able to move her out of the apartment, where she had been living with that man, and into our home in six hours. We took in a cat that my wife was allergic to, a springer spaniel dog that was in serious need of some behavioral modification, and my daughter with her craving for health food. I learned to hate the words, safflower oil, during that period of time. With her dog careening around the house and leaving me little greeting cards on the rug in the morning when I woke up, it was a real adventure.

But I trained that dog. I worked with it so much, so long, and so hard that before my daughter left, when I told that dog to "heal" she would jump up on your chest and put a paw on your forehead. What a dog! She would have fit in at Oral Roberts University.

After seven months of sowing the best we had into my daughter, she announced she was going to move across the state line into Wisconsin, because if she was to move out of state, she would have a better opportunity to get her driver's license back. I'm ashamed to admit, I thought, *Well, after all we've put into her, now she's going to leave and probably go back to working in the bars, begin drinking again, find some airhead for a boyfriend, and just repeat this cycle again.*

But Jeremiah 1:12 says that God hastens to perform His Word, and Isaiah 55:11 says, "So shall my word be that goeth forth out of my mouth: it shall not return unto me void." And during this time Wendy began to make a serious commitment to Jesus Christ. She began to take God's Word seriously. She began to learn who she was IN CHRIST. God's Word was beginning to take root and beginning to produce a return — some thirty, some sixty, and some a hundred-fold return (See Matthew 13:8).

Wendy moved to Lake Geneva, Wisconsin, a resort town, and went to work at a very large, successful restaurant called Popeye's that overlooks Lake Geneva. She found a one-room apartment, and there with her dog and cat she began to make an even more serious commitment to Christ. She found a little church in Delavin, Wisconsin, with a wonderful pastor by the name of Dave Hawley.

This church in Delavin challenged my daughter to a life of excellence. The pastor challenged her to show up early and qualify to turn over the overhead sheets on the projector. This meant she had to arrive an hour early in order to come for prayer and to organize everything. This led to an opportunity to work in the children's ministry, where in the last eighteen months prior to our beginning to write this book, she led over 100 children to a saving knowledge of the Lord Jesus Christ.

During this time, she began to develop a friendship with the pastor's son, Rob Hawley, a young man who loved God, and their friendship grew into a courtship. On Father's Day weekend, June 14, 1997, I had the privilege of walking my daughter down the aisle to marry Rob Hawley, a minister. Wendy's life had been restored from Satan's deceptions, lies, attacks, and plots of destruction. God's deliverance made possible this life-changing event for my daughter.

Going to war is never easy, but God's grace is sufficient. Be diligent and endure whatever comes your way. Keep your focus on the Lord, and don't let yourself be distracted by the affairs of this life. Remember in Whose army you are fighting and do whatever it takes to satisfy Him. Keep His battle plan always in front of you and fight according to His war manual — the Word. With it you will be complete, and it will keep you equipped for every situation you face.

Go back into the realm of the Spirit and pull back what the devil has stolen from you. Fight the good fight of faith and the Lord will stand with you and strengthen you. He will deliver you out of the mouth of the lion and from every evil work and preserve you for His heavenly kingdom.

Meditate on these scriptures:

> *For God has not given us a spirit of fear, but of power and of love and of a sound mind.*
>
> *2 Timothy 1:7* NKJV

> *You therefore must endure hardship as a good soldier of Jesus Christ.*
> *No one engaged in warfare entangles himself with the affairs of this life, that he may please him who enlisted him as a soldier.*
>
> *2 Timothy 2:3,4* NKJV

> *All Scripture is given by inspiration of God, and is profitable for doctrine, for reproof, for correction, for instruction in righteousness,*
> *That the man of God may be complete, thoroughly equipped for every good work.*
>
> *2 Timothy 3:16,17* NKJV

But the Lord stood with me and strengthened me…. I was delivered out of the mouth of the lion.

And the Lord will deliver me from every evil work and preserve me for His heavenly kingdom….

2 Timothy 4:17,18 NKJV

But the Lord God says, See, I am placing a Foundation Stone in Zion — a firm, tested, precious Cornerstone that is safe to build on. He who believes need never run away again.

Isaiah 28:16 TLB

Finally, my brethren, be strong in the Lord and in the power of His might.

Ephesians 6:10 NKJV

Therefore take up the whole armor of God, that you may be able to withstand in the evil day, and having done all, to stand.

Ephesians 6:13 NKJV

Trust in the Lord with all thine heart; and lean not unto thine own understanding.

In all thy ways acknowledge him, and he shall direct thy paths.

Proverbs 3:5,6

A wise man will hear, and will increase learning; and a man of understanding shall attain unto wise counsels.

Proverbs 1:5

Those who trust in the Lord are steady as Mount Zion, unmoved by any circumstance.

Just as the mountains surround and protect Jerusalem, so the Lord surrounds and protects his people.

Psalm 125:1,2 TLB

Q: How will you be proactive in waging war on the enemy?

Q: How has the enemy distracted you from the battle with the affairs of life, and what will you do to prevent this in the future?

Q: How has God shown you favor because you were honest and faced a situation head on?

Chapter 9

DISCERNING GOD-GIVEN RELATIONSHIPS

This is my commandment, That ye love one another, as I have loved you.

Greater love hath no man than this, that a man lay down his life for his friends.

Ye are my friends, if ye do whatsoever I command you.

John 15:12-14

Wow! What better friend could anyone have than Jesus? Can you comprehend it? Life is all about relationships — from birth to death. If we could get these three verses of Scripture down inside us and live them, we could eliminate most of today's problems. There would be no room for sorrow or worry or pain. Divorce would become obsolete. No longer would countries be destroyed by war. Jesus said if we would keep this commandment, we would have great joy.

These things I have spoken to you, that My joy may remain in you, and that your joy may be full.

John 15:11 NKJV

Created for Relationship

The Bible is the greatest book ever written about relationships. We were created for relationship. In the beginning of time God created us in His own image and gave man dominion over every living thing upon the earth. He made woman so that man would not be alone. He walked and talked with Adam and Eve in the Garden and enjoyed their fellowship.

> So God created man in his own image, in the image of God created he him; male and female created he them.
>
> And God blessed them, and God said unto them, Be fruitful, and multiply, and replenish the earth, and subdue it: and have dominion over the fish of the sea, and over the fowl of the air, and over every living thing that moveth upon the earth.
>
> Genesis 1:27,28

Just as man was deceived by Satan and disobeyed God in the Garden of Eden, destroying the very first relationship on earth, so has he continued to turn his back on the wisdom of the Ancient of Days and gone searching for wisdom in all the wrong places. Satan continues to lie to and deceive those who look outside of God's Word. He has practiced his deception for thousands of years, and he knows exactly what works. He's in the business of destroying relationships in families, friendships, businesses, churches, and countries. He especially delights in drawing people away from fellowship with their best Friend, Jesus.

In my speaking career, God has taken me to corporate America, to the sports world, and into the Christian sector. Wherever I go, people are begging for "quick fixes" to their problems or for any easy step-by-step, "how-to" process that will get them into the big leagues of wealth and fortune at whatever cost. I've seen the lives of talented, intelligent men and women destroyed by lust and greed for the things of this world. I've seen Christians living in defeat and misery because they don't know how to stand against the devil.

At one time, 70 percent of my speaking business was in the corporate market, and I believe God placed me there to bring His principles to this lost and dying generation. I learned it's true you can take a horse to water, but you can't make him drink. However, you can put salt in his oats and make him thirsty enough to drink.

I remember one time speaking to 16,000 network marketers in Great Britain. Before going to the platform to speak, the top executive called me aside and said, "This is not like our sister organization in America. We don't want any preaching here. Just tell us how to be in the best network in the whole universe." I said, "Right, got it."

I went out on that platform, waited for just the right time, and said, "Ladies and gentlemen, I'm in the best network in the whole universe. In my up-line, I've got Abraham, Isaac, and Jacob. My direct not only sponsored me, He died for me so I could be reconciled and hooked up with the Most High crown, double-diamond distributor — the Most High and Living God." The seed of the Word was planted into 16,000 people that night. There's always a way to give God the glory, whether it's a popular message or not. I'm commissioned to share the Good News and I leave the rest up to God.

The market for motivational speakers, books, and multimedia products has skyrocketed into a multimillion-dollar industry over the past twenty years. It's almost a guaranteed moneymaker for every famous Hollywood idol, retiring athlete, winning coach, Olympic gold medalist, Fortune 500 chief executive officer, and high-ranking military general or politician. Everybody has their book out there, marketing their formula as to how they got to the top.

Now I'm not saying we can't learn from those who have been successful, and there are some God-fearing men and women who are sharing His wisdom — people like Zig Ziglar, Charles "Tremendous" Jones, John

Maxwell, and Mary Kay Ash, who walk their Christian talk with integrity and honor. But many of today's "rich and famous" have been climbing the ladder of success only to find their ladder has been leaning against the wrong wall. It's possible to have everything and yet nothing without a relationship with God.

I've seen some of the greatest men in the sports world hit rock bottom and cry their eyes out — not for the riches they've lost, but because they've lost everyone who ever loved them. God has allowed me to counsel and pray with some of these famous people, and I can tell you the desire and need to be loved exists in every one of them. Without Jesus, Satan has robbed from them and lied to them, and all the fame and riches has not given them what they truly need and desire.

Finding God's Best

We can't deny we were created for relationship and fellowship, so how can we discern those relationships that are God-given? Let me share with you a most unusual story of how God taught me about such discernment. You see, love is not just words spoken with the mouth; it is a demonstration of the heart through obedience to His Word.

If anyone loves me, he will obey my teaching.
My Father will love him, and we will come to him
and make our home with him.

John 14:23 NIV

It was the summer of 1987. I had been divorced and a single parent since 1980. My son recently had gone to live with his mother, and I was living alone. I began to grow supernaturally lonely. I sensed it wasn't an attack of the enemy but rather that I was in a season of change. The Bible says in Proverbs 18:22 TLB, "The man who finds a wife finds a good thing; she is a blessing to him from the Lord." In Genesis 2:18 God said, "It is not good that man should be alone; I will make him an help meet for him." He also said in 1 Corinthians 7:9, "It is better to marry than to burn." I knew God was bringing me into a season of change, and He wasn't going to leave me to walk alone.

Unfortunately, I've been the kind of person who has always wanted to try to help God out. As I've grown older, and hopefully wiser, I've discovered that God doesn't need my help. You may be able to relate to what I'm saying, but the Scriptures say it best. He will show us His strength *if* we keep our hearts perfect toward Him.

For the eyes of the Lord run to and fro
throughout the whole earth, to shew himself strong in
the behalf of them whose heart is perfect toward him.

2 Chronicles 16:9

I had met a lady in Maryland by the name of Esther Dean. I was excited about meeting her because her nephew was Vernon Dean, the former starting defensive back for the Washington Redskins, and I wanted to invite him to a sports conference that I was involved in.

Esther Dean was a fascinating woman who had earned a Ph.D. in the field of education, but she didn't teach anywhere. What she did five days a week for six or seven hours a day was intercede for ministries. Upon meeting her she said, "I believe God wants to do something special in your life, I'm going to begin to pray for you." We talked from time to time by phone. She had a deep relationship with God, and occasionally God would use her to speak into my life.

In the summer of 1987 I said to myself, "This single life is not producing for me." I'd go to exciting singles' events like an "over the calf" sock count, a pigeon watch at the bank, or a Saturday afternoon at the local Sears store watching them unload a truckload of lawn and garden tools. Really exciting events. I thought to myself, *Surely God must have a wife for me — a second opportunity in life for a godly relationship.* With the door to reconciliation with my first wife closed and not to be opened again, it was time to move on.

God's Willing Helper

I thought, *Well, how am I going to go about finding a wife?* (Notice the "I" in that statement. I was about to help God out a bit!) Unfortunately, I approached it like the national football draft by picking out four nice ladies that I knew and prioritizing who would be my number one pick, my number two pick, number three pick, and number four pick. Pick number one was a lady from Dallas, Texas, who was visiting her mother for the summer up on Cape Cod.

I thought to myself, *I've never been to Cape Cod. I don't want to invest too much in this situation, but why not call United Airlines and get a free ticket from my Frequent Flyers' account. I'll fly up to the Boston area, see Cape Cod, and who knows, if this woman looks good in her aerobics outfit, her bathing suit, and owns a Bible, it could be God.* That was where my carnal Christianity was at that point in time.

I called up Esther Dean and said, "There's a lady that's up in the Boston area. I'm going to go up and visit her. Who knows, if she likes me, I like her, and the 'vibes' are good, there might be some relationship potential there." Esther Dean must have thought I was part Chinese — a

Chinese fellow by the name of "Sayfoo" — because she said to me, "Say fool, you're going to mess up your life, and not only that, you're going to mess up this woman's life. Neither of you will hit God's best. Now if you *really* want to know about your future and your destiny and the choice for a life's partner, get on your face before God and begin to pray." I hung up thinking, *So much for seeing Cape Cod!*

It was a hot July day in August 1987. I was Chaplain for the Chicago Cubs. So you will know that I'm a man of faith, the Cubs were the only team that year that could play a double-header and loose three games. If they got rained out, they'd have a victory rally. The crowds at Wrigley Field were so small, we didn't even bother to sing the national anthem at the start of the game.

Fifty of us would get down on home plate and sing, "Feelings." Harry Carey, the announcer, would come on the public address system and say, "Will the lady with the lost nine children please claim them, they're beating the Cubs 21-0." That was the year the Cubs found out what they had in common with the pop singer, Michael Jackson — they both wore gloves for no apparent reason. It was tough.

An Hour a Day

During a Bible study on prayer, I was trying to teach the Cubs from Larry Lea's book, *Could You Not Tarry One Hour?* In order to do this with some credibility, I tried to make sure I was the leading "prayer warrior" by spending an hour a day in prayer. Often an additional anointing would come on me for a nap. If I yielded to it, I would lay there checking my eyelids for holes, fall asleep, and drool on the carpet. But at least God knew my heart, and I was making an attempt.

I remember, on this particular day I had not taken time to pray. As I laid down on the floor of my office and thought about my "nonexistent plans for Saturday night," with a heart half filled with anger, I said, "God, Esther Dean from Maryland said that if I would ask You, You'd tell me who my wife is." It was not an audible voice, but it might as well have been, because coming up in my spirit I heard God say, "Yes, I have a wife for you, and her name is Doni Meeker from Tulsa, Oklahoma." This wasn't at all what I expected, or even wanted, to hear!

Say What, God?

I knew Doni. She was the bright, highly intelligent assistant to Keith Provance, President of Harrison House publishers. In my mind I saw Doni as a cross between Bible teachers Marilyn Hickey and Joyce Meyer, and I couldn't imagine anything that we could possibly have in common.

One day, as an act of kindness, purely from a business perspective and because she was my author representative at the publishing house, I had asked Doni if she would like to have lunch. She never looked up from her typewriter. She just moved the carriage ahead and said, "I see no good reason we should have lunch." I didn't need any more rejection, and I settled in my mind three important goals. One goal was to never milk a cobra. The second goal was to never get hit in the mouth with a hockey puck. And my third goal was to never spend any time with Doni Meeker in a social setting outside the context of business.

What a bummer to be laying on the floor and have God say, "I have a choice in life for you." I knew it was God. I knew it was undeniable, and I was angry. I got up off the floor, went to the local racquetball club, and drilled balls as low as possible to the floor and the wall, hitting what's known in racquetball as "kill shots" to deal with my anger.

You can imagine my surprise when on Tuesday I came into my office and there was a message that I was to call Doni at Harrison House publishers. I thought, *No problem, it's just something about my new book that's coming out,* Stay in the Game, *or my video,* Laughing Your Way to Excellence.

When I returned the call, the message I got as I spoke with Doni on the phone was this. She said, "On Monday night I was in prayer. During the second hour of prayer (which was difficult, if not impossible, for me to relate to) a spirit of intercession came on me, and the Lord gave me a word of knowledge concerning your ministry. I will be forwarding this word of knowledge to you in a memo."

I thought, *Yippee, that's exactly what I need and what I've been sitting on the edge of my seat waiting for* — *a memo from Doni.* I wasn't very talkative on the phone because I didn't want this sensitive, kind woman of God to hear me crying. Why was I crying? Because I knew God was moving in my life bringing my life's partner on the scene, and it wasn't happening my way.

It was October before we had our first date. Doni came to Chicago, and I proudly showed her Wheaton, Illinois, where I went to church, introduced her to my pastor, Van Gale, and took her by the beautiful Wheaton Oaks town homes which always caused me to cry. It sounds pretty crazy that someone would cry looking at a town home, but you have to understand I had lost everything. My credit, which had been sterling, was now X-rated. I, quite frankly, never thought I would ever own property again. When I saw people out in their yards cutting the grass and tending flowers, I used to weep because I thought that I had gone through a failure in life for which there was no recovery.

What Price Obedience?

We had our first date in October and a third date during the Christmas season. In the interim, while we began to build a relationship over the phone, Doni was going through her own struggles. She thought that to marry me would be an impossible task, an extremely difficult assignment, and she told God, "Enough is enough. I don't want to go through with this." God said this to her, "You're confusing two very different issues. Trust Me, love Van unconditionally, and don't confuse the two."

Why would God say that? Because after all the hurt and the rejection of my divorce, I really wasn't very "trustable," and Doni had every reason to pull out of the potential marriage. But she was obedient to her Lord, regardless of how impossible it looked in the natural. She had the faith to believe God was in control, and it would be okay.

We made a decision to obey God on January 25, 1988, in Tulsa, Oklahoma. Quite frankly, we both were scared. When I got to Tulsa, I thought, *Well, if we go ahead and do the "M" word — get married tonight — where will we stay?* I looked at my Frequent Flyer kit and sure enough I had a 50 percent discount coupon to stay at the Marriott Hotel. Doni went to the pastor's house with his wife to wait for me. I checked into the Marriott and spent some time lying before the Lord at Bedside Baptist with Pastor Pillow and Brother Sheets.

By the Mouth of Two Witnesses

At 6:30 that evening the pastor came over to counsel with me and to pray. As we knelt by the bed and prayed, it seemed like the prayer was taking forever. I thought, *If you don't hurry up and get to amen, I'm going to lose my courage and confidence to do this.* Then he said "I believe God is leading me to pray four things: 1) This marriage is going to be the best thing that ever happened to you, 2) God is going to prosper your marriage, 3) He is going to prosper you, and 4) He's going to prosper your wife."

I got up off my knees, went over to the sink, washed my face, put on some premarital aftershave lotion, and combed my hair. We went out into the hall to take the elevator down to the first floor. As we began to walk down that long hall of the Marriott Hotel, I could see a couple come around the corner walking hand-in-hand, arm-in-arm. Their profiles looked familiar, but I could not see their faces from that distance.

When I got closer it was Fort Worth-based Bible teachers, Kenneth and Gloria Copeland. I knew Rev. Copeland, because in 1981 he had come to speak to the Chicago Bear's football team when they had played the Dallas Cowboys in Dallas on Thanksgiving Day. He said, "Van, what are you doing here? Are you going to the same Bible seminar we're going to?" I said, "No, Kenneth, I'm getting married tonight." He said, "You've been single a long time, and I believe it is time." Then we began to talk about sports.

After a few minutes Gloria nudged him and said, "Kenneth, if we're going to be on time for the meeting, we need to leave now." He began to walk away. Then he came back and turned to me and said, "As a minister of the Gospel and a prophet of God, I need to say to you...God shows me that this marriage tonight is going to be the best thing that ever happened to you, that God is going to prosper your marriage, prosper you, and prosper your wife."

Kerplunk. I heard the pastor I was with bang up against the wall. He had sensed the power of God and heard this man, who just happened to walk down the same hall and whom he had never met before, repeat back to him what he had prayed in the room eight minutes earlier. God sent one of His choice servants to encourage me and to let me know I was on the right track and this marriage was of the Lord.

Even though we had little in common that night except the Lord, Doni and I were married. I found out that we did have one additional thing in common. Neither one of us had any money. We had a lot of enthusiasm, friendship, and a degree of love for each other, but no money — not even for a honeymoon.

Quick to Honor Obedience

But God is quick to honor obedience. While we were obeying God and being married, a major oil company,

Texaco, had called. When we got home to Chicago, I returned the call, and the Texaco representative said, "We are having a meeting of our Texaco Super Stars, men and women. We'd like for you to come to the Hyatt and speak to us." I assumed it was at the Hyatt Regency located at O'Hare Airport in Chicago. He said, "No, we're not going to Chicago in January. This meeting is being held on the island of Maui at the beautiful Hyatt Hotel. We would like you to come and speak for us. Bring your wife, and we will pay you well for your effort." One moment we had no money for a honeymoon, and the next moment we were on our way to the island of Maui, Hawaii.

While we were in Maui, Cigna Insurance called and said, "When you get back, would you please come to Disney World for a week? We'd like you to teach a morning seminar from 8:00-9:00, and then you'll have the rest of the day free at Disney World." Then we went on to PTL's Heritage USA in Charlotte, North Carolina, which was still in operation at that time. God gave us a one-month honeymoon and paid for it, with money left over. He's the God Who's more than enough. He's the God of Ephesians 3:20, Who is "able to do exceedingly abundantly above all that we ask or think."

God's Perfect Timing

Doni asked God why she should marry me and why it should be at this time. God impressed upon her that she needed to marry me at this time because if she did not, I would not make it through 1988. It truly was a difficult year.

After we were married in January of 1988, we made a decision that I would no longer be involved in the sports industry. This was a major change for me. I had had a heavy involvement in that industry for a number of years and probably was getting much, if not too much, of my self-esteem from the professional athletes I was hanging around with and the sports ministry I was doing. I believe God wanted to re-order my priorities and to give me "God-esteem," based on my relationship with Him.

In the summer of 1988 my father died, and I had to help my mother in the transition after his death. Also, we were living in close proximity to my former wife, which was causing a lot of strife. We felt the need to move, but as I alluded to earlier, due to the divorce, the emotional depression, and not working, my previously sterling credit rating had turned X-rated. I don't believe I could have bought a #2 pencil on credit, but God's man of faith and power decided it was time to move. We began to take the pictures off the walls and pack things, even though we had no idea where we were going.

A Woman of Faith

I thanked God for bringing into my life a woman of genuine faith who had a deep relationship with God and was far ahead of me spiritually in many areas. While I went back to Pennsylvania to help my mother clear up some matters after my father's death, Doni was led by the Spirit to go to a realtor and look at some properties. She said, "My husband liked those town homes that he showed to me in the fall, take me there."

Doni didn't put a limit on God. She looked at one, two, three places. The fourth house she walked into the Holy Spirit began to speak to her and said, "This is the place for you." It was beautifully carpeted, and it had the appliances she liked. Best of all, the attorney who owned the home had finished the basement as a corporate office from which he had operated his practice. Currently there were renters living in the home, and the owner wanted to get them out.

When I returned to Chicago, I went with Doni to look at this beautiful town home, but I felt like an absolute and complete fraud. It seemed like such a ridiculous exercise. At $150,000 it was priced far beyond anything I could conceive or believe. We had no money, and if they were to find out the Trans Union or TRW Credit rating, I couldn't imagine anybody loaning me anything for any reason. But this Baptist realtor who had more faith than I did said, "Why don't we approach the man?" I said, "That's ridiculous. Why waste his time? I have bad credit and no money." He said, "Well, if you go to a faith church, why don't you have some yourself!" Ouch, sometimes the truth hurts.

Divine Intervention

The realtor went to the owner and said, "Why don't we move these people in, let them have two years to make payments, and get a mortgage at the end of two years. They will give you the money they have today, and they will find the rest of the money by the end of twelve months to make a down payment on this town home." Miraculously by God's divine intervention, the owner agreed. We were able to scrape together $5,000 from my speaking fees. We moved in, signed a note, and gave the man $2,500 and an additional $2,500 for the closing.

I found a way to make those cold Chicago winters go by quickly. In Chicago it's so cold that every once in a while you'll see the Cook County politicians with their hands in their own pockets. It was so cold one morning I went out across the park and saw a couple of rabbits putting jumper cables on a beagle trying to get it started. It gets cold in Chicago, but when you have to come up with an extra $5,000 every ninety days and still pay all your bills, those days click off quickly and go by fast.

The Power of Agreement

Doni and I made a quality decision that we were going to take back what the enemy had stolen from us in the past. We went out and prayed and agreed in front of that home. We prayed, "Father, You said in Matthew 18:19 that if the two of us agree on earth as touching anything that we shall ask, You will do it for us, and we agree that this town home has been provided by Your hand, and we receive it in the name of Jesus."

We became radical and proactive in our faith. Yes, we spoke to that mountain of debt, that mountain of house payments, and said, "Be paid. Debt be removed and cast into the sea." We would not doubt in our hearts, but believed that those things which we said would come to pass and we would own that town home.

We continued to stand on the Word together and to give generously to God.

> *Give, and it shall be given unto you; good measure, pressed down, and shaken together, and running over, shall men give into your bosom. For with the same measure that ye mete withal it shall be measured to you again.*
>
> Luke 6:38

> *And Jesus answered and said, Verily I say unto you, There is no man that hath left house, or brethren, or sisters, or father, or mother, or wife, or children, or lands, for my sake, and the gospel's, but*

he shall receive an hundredfold now in this time, houses, and brethren, and sisters, and mothers, and children, and lands, with persecutions; and in the world to come eternal life.

Mark 10:29,30

We stood on His promises that if we give for the Gospel's sake, we will receive a hundred-fold return, not in the sweet by-and-by, but in this life. We continued to give to God and believe God for the increase. Within twelve months God sent us not only the money for the down payment but the remaining $15,000 we needed to complete our contract. Also during that period of time God began to supernaturally restore my credit. Doni had excellent credit and wonderful administrative abilities, and when we combined those factors with the restoration of my credit, within two years God gave us an excellent mortgage. Now we own that home.

We are able to say, as of the writing of this book, we have never been late or missed a payment. God has allowed us the adventure and excitement of living by faith. God has shown Himself to be faithful, and when we give to Him, we believe Him. When we speak the Word of God into the situations of life, He will show up. God will pay the bills, and we are believing God to own our home free and clear with supernatural debt reduction.

Obedience and Blessings

When I obeyed God, honored Doni's giftings and direction, and quit demanding God to give me my *wants*, but rather started receiving from Him my *needs*, then God was able to bring me His best. But in order to receive God's hand-chosen, lifetime partner for me, I had to get out of the flesh and learn to live according to the Spirit, to hear from God, and let God pick my mate. His choice far exceeded what I would have chosen. And although it has not always been easy, it has been extremely rewarding.

God created us all for relationship. Learn to discern the relationships God has chosen for you in your personal life, at work, and in the Church. If Satan has been robbing you of these relationships, draw a line in the sand today and call a halt to the devil's plan. Don't be moved by your emotions or the lust of the flesh any longer.

Pray and ask God to reveal His perfect will for you, and then listen to God's voice carefully. Ask the Holy Spirit to confirm what you are hearing in the Word with specific scriptures and by the mouth of godly witnesses. Apply the Word in every situation so you won't be deceived. Seek godly counsel and prayer. Walk in love and in obedience, and let Jesus' light shine through you. And always do what Jesus commanded us to do — love one another as He has loved us!

Meditate on these scriptures:

The Lord God hath given me the tongue of the learned, that I should know how to speak a word in season to him that is weary.

Isaiah 50:4

Let nothing be done through strife or vainglory; but in lowliness of mind let each esteem other better than themselves.

Philippians 2:3

Most of all, let love guide your life, for then the whole church will stay together in perfect harmony.

Colossians 3:14 TLB

And the Lord make you to increase and abound in love one toward another.

1 Thessalonians 3:12

And the servant of the Lord must not strive; but be gentle unto all men, apt to teach, patient.

2 Timothy 2:24

Be kindly affectioned one to another with brotherly love; in honour preferring one another.

Romans 12:10

And five of you shall chase an hundred, and an hundred of you shall put ten thousand to flight: and your enemies shall fall before you by the sword.

Leviticus 26:8

Moreover if thy brother shall trespass against thee, go and tell him his fault between thee and him alone: if he shall hear thee, thou hast gained thy brother.

Matthew 18:15

A man that hath friends must shew himself friendly: and there is a friend that sticketh closer than a brother.

Proverbs 18:24

A good name is rather to be chosen than great riches, and loving favour rather than silver and gold.

Proverbs 22:1

Q: How do you see the love of the Father demonstrated in the God-given relationships in your life?

Q: How do you show this love to others who come across your path each day?

Q: What is the most important thing you have learned about godly relationships from someone who has been a role model for you?

Q: What do you plan to do differently from this day forward in discerning your God-given relationships?

Chapter 10

PUTTING FIRST THINGS FIRST

You shall have no other gods before Me.

You shall not bow down to them nor serve them.

For I, the LORD your God, am a jealous God, visiting the iniquity of the fathers upon the children to the third and fourth generation of those who hate Me,

But showing mercy to thousands, to those who love Me and keep My commandments.

Deuteronomy 5:7,9,10 NKJV

We do serve a jealous God, and He will not tolerate His people worshipping other gods. But more importantly, what the above scriptures reveal to us is how God ordained the family to carry His life to future generations. Another scripture that reinforces this is found in Deuteronomy 7:9 NKJV:

Therefore know that the Lord your God, He is God, the faithful God who keeps your covenant and mercy for a thousand generations with those who love Him and keep His commandments.

Is it any wonder that Satan's first line of attack was against Adam and Eve's relationship with the Father, with each other, and then against their first seed, Cain and Abel? This proves what a threat a God-ordained marriage is to Satan and reinforces how critical it is for us to keep our priorities in line with God's order for our lives. We have an awesome responsibility to our spouses and to our children to walk in righteousness so that our present and future generations will walk in blessings and not curses.

The marriage ceremony abounds with joy and promises of love. It seals a covenant of commitment similar to the commitment we make with God when we make a decision to follow Christ. When the ceremony is over, the couple then must walk out their commitment over the course of a lifetime.

The ceremony is a beginning, but the building of a loving relationship requires sacrifice, endurance, patience, long-suffering, dedication, and strength of character. It is not easily attained, but the refining growth process — as painful as it is — produces the pure gold of true commitment. So too is the maturing process which we go through in building our relationship with our heavenly Father.

His Divine Order

God's divine order is for us to give Him our worship and attention first, then to give to our spouse, and then to our inner circle relationships of family, ministry, business, or whatever is close to our hearts and callings. In the last chapter we examined how to discern God-given relationships. We briefly touched on the fact that the very first attack from Satan came to destroy man's relationship with God.

That may have been thousands of years ago, but Satan hasn't changed his first line of attack or his tactics. His first priority is still to draw us away from our relationship with the Father through deception and distraction. His second priority is then to attack our marriage relationships, and thirdly to attack us through those relationships that make up the inner circle of our lives.

We must remain on alert to such attacks, have our weapons sharpened and ready, and put on our spiritual armor daily. Our primary battle plan must be to keep first things first in our daily priorities — our time with God, our time with our spouse, and then our time with our inner circle.

Considering all that I just shared, it should not have come as any surprise to Doni and me what kind of battle we would be facing. It has not been easy. We have faced a lot of turmoil with our blended family. We've had to deal with my lack of leadership in the home and not knowing how to be an effective husband. God had to hit me over the head to teach me it requires a commitment of time to build an intimate, loving relationship with my wife and with Him.

But thank God, we don't have to be embarrassed to ask for help, and there's plenty of help available. One of the things that has made a difference in our life was writing *Today's Family* in Branson, Missouri, and buying Dr. Gary Smalley's excellent video series, "Love Is a Decision." In it he teaches the difference between men and women — their physiological differences and the way they communicate differently.

Just like the popular best-seller *Men Are From Mars and Women Are From Venus* says, men and women communicate in very different and unique ways. We need to let God show us how to communicate with one another and meet one another's needs.

A Commanded Blessing

Doni and I are not where we want to be or need to be yet, but we have come a long way in these past ten years. Now we are seeking, even in a modest effort, to have the unified vision that Psalm 133 speaks about, for that is where the commanded blessing is. This speaks of the unity the Lord wishes for us to have in all relationships.

Behold, how good and pleasant it is for brethren to dwell together in unity!

*It is like the precious ointment upon the head,
that ran down the beard, even Aaron's beard: that
went down to the skirts of his garments;*

*As the dew of Hermon, and as the dew that
descended upon the mountains of Zion: for there the
Lord commanded the blessing, even life for evermore.*

Psalm 133

Doni and I want to share with you where we have
walked these past ten years in the hopes it will spare you
some of the pain we have endured. There is great wisdom
in learning from other's mistakes.

Key Relationships

Shortly after our marriage in 1988, God began to
move us out of the corporate world, out of eighteen years
in the insurance industry with New York Life and
Northwestern Mutual. I also began to phase out of the
professional sports ministry, having served as Chaplain for
the Chicago Bears, the Chicago Cubs, the Chicago White
Sox and speaking to many of the visiting pro teams.

It was a time of great excitement. God began to open
up ministry from one end of the nation to the other, from
Canada to Mexico. Our ministry was growing faster than
we could imagine. But as so often happens to people in
ministry and in business, the demanding schedule, the
desire to develop better material for presentations and

preaching, and the desire to develop a first-class organization soon took its toll. We became caught up in the busyness of it all.

Those key relationships — relationship with God, relationship with your spouse, and then our relationship with our inner circle of family, ministry, and career — began to get out of order. We were doing things *for* God as opposed to spending time *with* God. The time we were spending in ministry doing for others, doing for family, attempting to put together a very difficult blended family situation, soon left us drained, short of energy, and at times short of temper and patience.

From 1988 to the eve of 1998, we developed many positive strengths. We had an outstanding and effective nationwide ministry with many return engagements and follow-up bookings. There was a high demand for our services without any significant promotion or sales/marketing campaign. The professionalism, integrity, and excellence of our services were unquestionable. We were building relationships and networking very effectively, and we were busy.

But many times we were busy doing the wrong thing. While we were effective professionally, our personal relationships were suffering. Our ministry had become very labor intensive. There was a lack of time with God and the potential for burnout loomed heavily on the horizon.

The intensity and pressures grew so quickly after we were married, that Doni and I never really had the opportunity to get to know each other's ways or how to work together in unity. She had an analytical personality, and I had an expressive personality. Our personalities had the potential to just absolutely rub each other the wrong way and drive each other up the wall, like sandpaper grinding against the roughest wood.

We began to lose our effectiveness at flowing together personally and professionally. We did not have a unified vision. We began to wonder and waver about where we should be located, what our church home should be, and how to run the ministry. We even found ourselves limiting God. As it says in Psalm 78:41, "Yea, they turned back and tempted God, and limited the Holy One of Israel." We started to experience a decrease in our finances as our growth potential was limited to my time on the road. All this caused a corresponding decrease in regular, meaningful communication with Doni and with God.

Thank God, we knew enough to seek out some godly counsel and help. Since 1990 we have had an excellent relationship with and serve on the Board of World Harvest Church in Columbus, Ohio, where Rod Parsley is the senior pastor. In the course of this relationship we met an outstanding couple, Dean and Carol Radtke. Dean had served the Avon Company out of Manhattan,

New York, and then later The Limited Company out of Columbus, Ohio. He was a trouble-shooter. He had gone to Bible school at World Harvest Bible College and had been the chief operating officer at World Harvest Church for six years. Dean then moved out into the consulting field and worked with visionaries to help them facilitate their goals and plans. I called Dean and asked him to come and help us.

God's Partnership

Dean has a high level of God-given discernment, and he immediately began to bore in on the problems. Our priorities had reversed themselves from God's divine order. He said the chief executive officer — yours truly — needed to spend concerted time in regular prayer, Bible study, and listening to the God he serves. He pointed out that it is an issue of relationships. He said, "You are in a partnership. God is the general partner, and He is the one Who put up most of the resources and sacrifice. Yes, He sacrificed His Son, Jesus Christ. You are Van Crouch, the limited partner, literally. You are limited, and without drawing on the forces of God as the general partner, the fact is, this ministry is going to come to a screeching halt." He pointed out we have a convenant contract in which we are not supposed to operate without the approval of God, His direction, and His counsel. He said there needed to be an immediate re-ordering of priorities and working on relationships.

We had allowed the ministry to come first, and then under that, ministry to our family. We had a blended family. I had a son with special needs and a daughter who was being restored. Doni had a son and a daughter who were getting started in marriage with a number of needs, and we had given so much and so often to others, we had not given to ourselves.

Dean said to me, "You have placed your ministry as number one, your spouse as second, and then the time you are spending with God is coming in third. The results of spending more time with God and building this relationship supernaturally will address all the needs identified — peace and unity in all relationships, a deeper and more fulfilling ministry, personal strength, a market, and product ideas.

Operating on Credit

Dean Radtke got to the meat of the matter when he said, "Van, you have hit the self-effort ceiling personally, in your marriage, and in the ministry." Then he made a dramatic statement that caught my attention. He said, "You are operating on credit with God. You have been doing many things up to now without adequate intimacy, worship, prayer, Bible study, and listening. But for God to continue to bless your ministry in the way the priorities are arranged presently would be for God to go against His character and against His Word." Matthew 6:33 says, "Seek ye first the kingdom of God, and his righteousness; and all these things shall be added unto you." Dean explained that this misalignment of priorities is prevalent in all of us at times. It's when we take it to the extreme that God has to step in and get our attention. He certainly had mine!

At times I was overwhelmed with hopelessness, feeling that we would never grow, that our marriage relationship was in trouble, wondering how our children would ever be restored. Dean pointed out to me as I need to point out to you, Jesus died for our every situation. I needed to literally praise God in the situation as it was, as it is, and invite Him into it. He immediately inhabits the praises of His people.

I needed to quit honoring the enemy by focusing on what he said about the situation or my wife or my family. I needed to learn to focus on my wife's gifts, strengths, abilities, and to help her more by hindering her less. The fact was, I could not organize a one-car funeral or lead a retreat. I needed to get out of our office and quit bringing confusion into the operations. I needed to work on the 20 percent that produces the 80 percent of productivity.

As the Italian economist Pareto, said: "There is an inverse law of production — 20 percent of our input will give us 80 percent of our output." I was dabbling in things that I was not equipped to do. My wife said to me, "I already have a father. I don't need a second father. I'm not trying out for the team. I do not need a coach. I need a friend. I need a confidant. I need a companion. I need a lover. We need to go back to the fundamentals of building this relationship."

It is possible for a highly focused man in ministry or business to drive his wife away without trying. We wake up one morning and ask where have all the feelings gone. I was learning that if my wife does not win first place in my life, then I lose. She needed a shoulder to lean on, not a mouth to direct her.

Like a spaceship moving through the heavens, our marriage is subject to laws that determine whether or not it will be a success or failure. If any of these laws are violated, then my wife and myself are locked into orbits destined to crash. However, if during the marriage and the relationship I'll recognize which law or principle I have violated and make the necessary adjustments, my marriage would get better and stay on the right course.

A Very Difficult Assignment

When I first met Doni at Harrison House publishers, I asked her what was her course in life. As a single woman she said to me, "God is preparing me for a difficult assignment." We now can look back and laugh at this statement. How true it was. What a difficult assignment to enter into a marriage with a man who had a lot of extra emotional baggage, who was suffering from rejection, not only from a divorce, but possibly passed down through the generations of the family.

We already read in Deuteronomy that the sins of the father are visited on the children up to the fourth generation. And then add to this picture two people coming together out of failed marriages, with a great deal of hurt and all the pressures of a blended family situation, without the leader knowing much about how to love his wife. That would be enough to discourage almost anyone.

We really do want to love our spouse. Some of us, who have not experienced loving relationships in our families, just don't know how. We've not had any successful examples to follow. Our parents often did the best they could, but they were attempting to operate long before Focus on the Family with James Dobson and Gary Smalley and many other excellent family organizations, counselors, or specialists in the areas of relationship came along.

Three Kinds of Love

I had to learn that there are three essential kinds of love. One is companionship, and we are to enjoy just being together, investing time together, spending time together. We need to have genuine companionship. We also need to have passion to build our emotions above the companionship level toward one another and then move on to genuine love. Genuine love allows me to see a need in my wife and then to have the privilege of actually meeting it.

Immaturity on the part of one or both of the partners can open up the relationship to many destructive forces, such as fear, which results when we imagine or perceive that our needs and goals will not be met. Loneliness is another force which results from dependence on other people for our happiness and expecting some human being to meet our needs — needs that can be met only in a relationship with God through His Son, Jesus Christ.

Anger is a powerfully destructive force when it is brought into a marriage. It may be from a failed relationship or from something that has happened to us during childhood. Wherever it comes from, it often causes inner turmoil and frustration when we cannot control people or control our circumstances.

Envy is another force which springs up from a desire to possess what someone else has. We imagine that if we gain what he or she has, then we will be happy. Coming along hand in hand with envy is jealousy, which is caused by a fear of losing something or someone of value because our needs are not met.

Selfishness is the motivation behind all these forces. We have people pulling on us, family members pulling on us, we feel like an automatic teller machine where people step up and push a button and say, "I want to talk, come here, come there, pay this bill, help me meet this need, write this book." These forces put a tremendous strain on a marriage.

I had to make a concerted effort to learn what my wife's needs were, so she and I could be in harmony together through a deeper, more intimate relationship. I had to learn that she needs companionship, harmony, and a feeling of togetherness. She had to know that she is valued in my life — more important than my mother or any of our children or our friends or our secretary or our ministry. I also had to learn that when she is hurting she needs to know that I am willing to share an intimate moment of comfort without demanding an explanation or giving one of those famous Crouch lectures or a locker room pep talk.

Becoming a Promise Keeper

Doni needed open and unobstructed communication. (Men, note that this is a primary need for all women. It is part of their nature.) She needed to be praised so she could feel she was a valuable part of my life. She needed to feel free to help me without fearing retaliation or anger or that nobody could do it quite like Van. She needed to know that I would be loyal to her and defend her and protect her. Doni needed to know that her opinion is so valuable that I would discuss decisions with her, including

decisions about giving to other ministries, decisions about
the direction of our ministry, and act only after carefully
evaluating her advice. She needed to know that she could
share her life with me in every area, home and family and
outside interests. She needed to know that I would be the
kind of man her son could follow and her daughter would
want to marry.

Doni also needed to know that I would tenderly hold
her and be near to her apart from times of sexual
intimacy, that I simply loved being with her, holding her,
talking to her, taking her counsel, and building a relationship. This doesn't make a man a wimp. This makes a man
develop the characteristics promoted by a nationally
known organization that is impacting America —
Promise Keepers. Yes, I am a man of God and because of
God's promises to me as a man, I can keep my promises
and commitments to my wife and family and order my
priorities aright.

Feelings Are Okay

In the areas of relationship I had to learn that feelings
are not wrong. Feelings are who you are at that point in
time. Feelings are not to be contested; they are to be
understood. They are not to be judged, but heard and
considered. To be in touch with our feelings is critical.
Understanding our own response to situations enables us
to judge ourselves rightly, allowing God to show us what

is appropriate and inappropriate as we strive to be more like Christ. We must stop blaming others for our feelings and expecting someone else to change the way we feel and then to do something about it. We must evaluate our response to situations and evaluate the corresponding behavior and actions.

When I became more aware of my feelings, I was able to share them with God and with my wife. We become more intimate in both relationships. We become more sensitive to feelings. The fact is, feelings are real, and they do need to be considered. However, I thank God for the integrity of His Word, which says we're not to be moved by how we feel but by His Word.

Back to the Foundation

As Dean Radtke helped us focus on our priorities and deal with issues in our relationships, it became obvious that Doni and I had both adopted coping behaviors from previous relationships with family and spouses, and those coping behaviors were not appropriate for our relationship now. We had to go back down to the very foundation and start exercising the fruits of the spirit — humility, patience, forgiveness — and not dumping on each other with anger, rejection, silence, or guilt trips. We had to forgive and let go and move on from the past. We had to stop trying to control and change each other and let God show us individually what each of us needed to change in our own behavior. He will tell us what to change in ourselves when we ask Him.

As someone who enjoys being around people, and my wife being more introverted, Doni has said many times she felt like she was living in a house with no locks and anybody could come and take whatever they wanted whenever they wanted. Most of our focus was on crisis, and we moved from one crisis to the next. As a leader, I had to put into or invest into her life. I was not to treat her like a child treats his mother, expecting her to meet my needs. I was to love her unconditionally, and I should be the one sowing into her.

In the area of respect, I tended to give it and then turn around and take it away. She felt as though she was always having to prove herself, and I was living on credit, not only with God having my priorities out of order, but I was not consistent with her. I had not taken the responsibility as the head — the leader — in our home.

Yes, I was speaking around the country on how to be effective in leadership, but I wasn't being effective in my own home. I often made the statement in my presentations that many men come home and drop off their body, and their mind goes somewhere else. The lights are on but there's nobody home. They are emotionally or mentally absent. I was guilty of this myself.

Invest in Each Other

We simply were not taking time to build our relationship. "Vacation" was a word that was not in our vocabulary. Most vacations had speaking engagements attached to them. Yes, it was only an eighteen-minute speaking assignment or a midweek service somewhere, but it broke the flow of our vacation time together.

At that time God was saying, "Pull back, invest in each other; do not go out and minister. Your ministry is to one another. Set priorities. Open the Bible. Get your nose in the Book. Spend time praying together as a couple. Refresh yourselves, and let someone else speak into your life." One of the reasons our relationship was in trouble was that there was not the proper investment of time.

The Right to be Different

I had to learn that my wife had the right to be different. She had a right to her opinion, and I was not to dump on her, expecting her to be God in my life and meet all my emotional needs. I had to carry the leadership. A leader is simply someone who goes ahead and does what has to be done before it has to be done.

I needed to value her, notice her during the day, stop by for a hug with no other motivation or any sexual connotation. (Dr. Gary Smalley says that due to the chemical, testosterone, a man thinks about sex every 48 seconds. Personally, I've gone as long as a minute and a half.)

It was important to simply stop for a moment, ask her how she's doing — and then actually *listen* to her! I had to honor and think the best about her. I had to keep our private life and private business to myself and not expose it to a nationwide network of support people. I needed to show respect in public *and* in private and to treat her as special.

God's Secret Agent

But the greatest revelation I had was realizing that my wife is actually a secret agent sent by God. Someway, somehow in eternity past God saw some potential in my life. But I would not have fulfilled my potential, not achieved my destiny, if God had not sent her into my life to motivate me, to be the catalyst that would cause me to go to the next level.

I had to fight the battle in my mind. I had to take some time off, not only to invest with God, but to invest with my wife. Then we had to build a new level of trust and confidence in one another.

Many people do not realize, when they cross the line and go into ministry, it will not be done uncontested. Speaker Joyce Meyer says that reaching a new level in your life will produce a new devil. No, he's not recreated, but he has new strategies, new deceptions, and new distractions to try to kill, steal, and destroy you.

The devil hates good relationships. He fears me having a productive relationship with my wife, because the Bible says that our agreement multiples our power and impact. We cannot afford to operate in strife. It opens up the door to the devil. We needed to kick strife out, spiritually cleanse our house, and realize we overcome by the blood of the Lamb and the word of our testimony.

God's Vote of Confidence

When we put our relationship in order, God can bless what we are putting our hands to. Then God can say, "Now I have a vote of confidence in you, in our relationship and our ministry, and therefore, I will bless you, I will provide for you, I will send you to My choice places of ministry and assignment because you are in obedience to Me and My Word."

In our situation we came to the fundamental truth that Christ is the answer. In John 14:6 He said, "I am the way, the truth, and the life." He was saying, "I am the way to God, I am the truth to be learning and the life to be living." In God's Word there are answers to everything we need to know. He is the Master consultant, the Master psychologist — not me — not anyone but Jesus.

A Godly Covering

I had to go back and make a concerted effort to exhort my wife, to edify her, and we needed to forgive one another. Then I needed to draw closer to God and get under the blood of His protection and in complete submission to Him. I had to take my rightful place in the headship of our home, to cover my wife in prayer, with kindness, with praise, and with love. You see, God was not ready to bless our ministry until we dealt with the deficiencies within our relationships — first our relationship with Him and then our relationship with each other.

When I got serious about getting my priorities back into godly order, I experienced the most phenomenal thing. We operate our ministry by living by faith. We believe that promotion comes from God, and He will make a place for us and bring us before great men.

> *For exaltation comes neither from the east nor from the west nor from the south.*
>
> *But God is the Judge: He puts down one, And exalts another.*
>
> Psalm 75:6,7 NKJV

> *A man's gift makes room for him, And brings him before great men.*
>
> Proverbs 18:16

I do not believe I am to sit on the phone attempting to convince corporations, trade associations, great churches, or professional sports teams to call me and offer me speaking engagements. I found that the secret is to praise and worship God, to seek Him, to spend time with Him, and spend time with my spouse. As I began to delve into the Word of God, into the fundamentals of building a successful relationship, God began to give us almost more places to go than we could handle. Jesus went where He was celebrated, not tolerated, and I know I'm not the right speaker or minister for every place, every situation, or every church. But when I let God fill my schedule, when I order my priorities right, God began to move in my life at a new level and do exceedingly abundantly above all I could ask or think and show Himself strong in my life.

Discover Your "Yes" in Life

The keys to a blessed life are relationship, setting priorities, and discovering your "Yes" in life. Know what you're called to do, and know what you're *not* called to do. Seek first the kingdom of God and His righteousness, and then God will keep His Word. He'll watch over His Word and hasten to perform it. He will send you where He wants you. He will provide, because where there is ministry there is money with which to do it. With His vision comes provision. Where there is no vision, the people perish; but where there is no provision, the vision perishes. When God has called you and sent you, He will pay the bill.

Doni and I have opened up our lives to you in such a personal way because we want to help you and those you love to find joy and peace in your relationships. We know that we are not unique and that many of you may be struggling with hurts from the past or with any number of crises in your lives. We pray that our testimony will encourage you to reevaluate your priorities and to "put first things first" — your relationship with your loving, heavenly Father, your relationship with your spouse, and then your relationship with your inner circle. Seek wisdom and counsel from His Word and stand on His promises. Allow repentance and forgiveness to bring healing to your hearts; and remember yesterday is gone, and tomorrow may never come, but you've still got today. Make it count! Take back the ground the enemy has stolen from you in your relationships and walk in unity with the Father, with your spouse, and with all others.

Meditate on these scriptures.

Finally, all of you be of one mind, having compassion for one another; love as brothers, be tenderhearted, be courteous;

Not returning evil for evil or reviling for reviling, but on the contrary blessing, knowing that you are called to this, that you may inherit a blessing.

1 Peter 3:8,9 NKJV

Above all things have fervent love for one another, for love will cover a multitude of sins.

1 Peter 4:8 NKJV

Wives, likewise, be submissive to your own husbands, that even if some do not obey the word, they, without a word, may be won by the conduct of their wives.

1 Peter 3:1 NKJV

Likewise you husbands, dwell with them with understanding, giving honor to the wife, as to the weaker vessel, and as being heirs together of the grace of life, that your prayers may not be hindered.

1 Peter 3:7 NKJV

There is no fear in love; but perfect love casts out fear, because fear involves torment. But he who fears has not been made perfect in love.

We love Him because He first loved us.

1 John 4:18,19 NKJV

For where envy and self-seeking exist, confusion and every evil thing will be there.

But the wisdom that is from above is first pure, then peaceable, gentle, willing to yield, full of mercy and good fruits, without partiality and without hypocrisy.

Now the fruit of righteousness is sown in peace by those who make peace.

James 3:16-18 NKJV

Let us therefore come boldly to the throne of grace, that we may obtain mercy and find grace to help in time of need.

Hebrews 4:16 NKJV

For God has not given us a spirit of fear, but of power and of love and of a sound mind.

2 Timothy 1:7 NKJV

Wives, submit to your own husbands, as is fitting in the Lord.

Husbands, love your wives and do not be bitter toward them.

Colossians 3:18,19 NKJV

That their hearts may be encouraged, being knit together in love, and attaining to all riches of the full assurance of understanding, to the knowledge of the mystery of God, both of the Father and of Christ,

In whom are hidden all the treasures of wisdom and knowledge.

Colossians 2:2,3 NKJV

Don't think only of yourself. Try to think of the other fellow, too, and what is best for him.

1 Corinthians 10:24 TLB

For though I am free from all men, I have made myself a servant to all, that I might win the more.

I have become all things to all men, that I might by all means save some.

Now this I do for the gospel's sake, that I may be partaker of it with you.

1 Corinthians 9:19,22,23 NKJV

Q: What specific steps do you plan to take to set your priorities in godly order?

Q: What relationship can you identify that needs to be strengthened or restored?

Q: How do you plan to change your attitude or behavior to bring about this restoration?

Chapter 11

IRON SHARPENS IRON

As iron sharpens iron, so one man sharpens another.
Proverbs 27:17 NIV

God's Word instructs us over and over to be humble and to subject ourselves one to another. If we don't provide caution, loving correction, or warnings when we see someone else headed for trouble, who will do it for us? Such accountability is critical to destroy the enemy's tricks and deceptions. Loving, constructive criticism helps keep our hearts pure. Those we love and who care about us often have insights into us that we don't have ourselves.

Life's Board of Directors

I'll never forget Jim Sundberg, one of the greatest catchers in the history of major league baseball. After one of the Cub's games in Chicago, I asked if he wanted to go get some dinner. He said, "No, I've got a meeting with my Life's Board of Directors."

I said, "Who?"

"My Life's Board of Directors."

I said, "What's that?"

He said, "I have some people who really care about me and my life. We go out to dinner once a quarter, and before the dessert comes, they look me in the eye and ask me how I'm doing and how I'm doing in my life. They ask what my relationship is with God, with my wife, and with our children."

Dr. Charles Swindoll, the great evangelical preacher, tells a similar story about his days as a pastor. One of the elders in his church would come to him every six weeks and say, "Charles, how's your relationship with God? How's your relationship with your wife and children? Are you in the Word of God? Charles, are you praying? Are you contemplating having an affair with any woman in this church? Charles, have you lied about any of these questions?"

You see, you're nobody until somebody expects something of you. If you want to take back the ground the enemy has stolen from you and keep that ground, you must choose to be accountable.

Insist on Integrity

We all need a group of loving, godly people to help hold us up when we are weak, to pray with us and for us, and to give wise counsel and guidance when needed. If you've got a pastor or somebody in your life who holds you accountable and helps keep you focused, you have somebody who cares for you. And just as they help you stay focused, you need to be sure they are living godly lives and their fruit is good and acceptable to the Lord.

Insist on integrity for yourself and for those with whom you surround yourself.

> *Judge me, O Lord; for I have walked in mine integrity: I have trusted also in the Lord; therefore I shall not slide.*
>
> *Examine me, O Lord, and prove me; try my reins and my heart.*
>
> *I have hated the congregation of evildoers; and will not sit with the wicked.*
>
> *But as for me, I will walk in mine integrity: redeem me, and be merciful unto me.*
>
> Psalm 26:1,2,5,11

A number of years ago a man by the name of Napoleon Hill wrote a runaway bestseller, a book titled *Think and Grow Rich*. In this book he comments on the power of the mastermind group. This is similar to Jim Sundberg's Life's Board of Directors. I believe that to go higher you've got to surround yourself with people who are going somewhere in life.

Big Dogs Have Big Fleas

I was in a Bible study with Paul Harvey back in the days when I lived in Oak Park, Illinois. For about five or six years Paul and I attended the same church, and every Sunday morning at 6:30, we would get together for a Bible study. Paul Harvey said to me one time, "Van, if you want to get big fleas, you've got to hang out with big dogs."

That's a cute little one-liner, but what it means is that you've got to involve yourself with people who are going to the next level, going higher, deeper in God, who are motivated and excited. If I'm a number five on a scale of one to ten and want to be a ten, then I've got to hang around with some nines and tens to move up the ladder and to become more effective. I've got to spend time with people who will change my life, challenge my thinking, and yes, even hold me accountable.

Stay Away From Mr. Gloom and Doom

I found out that in my life I've got to eliminate those people who have mental BO, the light comes on when they leave the room. That means never share a God-inspired idea at a family picnic with Uncle Frank who is on relief and views the fifth grade as his senior year or wants to use his fishing license as a form of valid identification. His side of the family tree doesn't work, and he's going to try to attempt to talk me out of what God said I could do, what God said I could be, what God said I could have. He wants to talk about what passed away, won't work anymore, somebody else who had the same sickness, the same disease, or went into the same business and failed. He is Mr. Gloom and Doom! As I said, he's got mental BO.

Zig Ziglar probably says it best when he says, "People who have stinkin' thinkin' need a checkup from the neck up to prevent hardening of the attitudes." These people will pull you down rather than up.

Invest Wisely

For a number of years I was chaplain of the Chicago Bears. We had a number of outstanding players, including a great defensive tackle by the name of Dan Hampton who had played at the University of Arkansas. Dan could lay on his back and bench press 400 to 500 pounds. I've often used this illustration. If I put Dan on a table about eight feet high and told him to try to pull me up while I try to pull him down, because of the law of leverage and the law of gravity, even with his great strength, I've got a better chance of pulling him down than he does of lifting me up.

The point is, many people in life will pull you down rather than lift you up. You've got to eliminate them from your life to go higher. That does not mean you're to be aloof, cold, and stop reaching out to others. But to go higher, you've got to eliminate the cop-outs, the dropouts, and the burn outs and invest your time with some people who will go all out.

I have some people in my own life — Rod Parsley, Senior Pastor of World Harvest Church, Columbus, Ohio; Dr. Jim Zirkle of Living Waters Ministry; Dave Blunt, Pastor of Church on the Rock, St. Peter's,

Missouri; Sherman Owens from Sarasota, Florida, Victory Family Center; and Dean Radtke of Radtke & Associates, Scottsdale, Arizona — who regularly speak into my life.

These men and their wives invest time looking at our ministry, looking at our relationships, and meeting with Doni and me to help us develop our relationship both personally and professionally in order to grow to the next level. They help us to crystallize our vision, to see where we want to go, and then show us how to facilitate our getting there. This kind of iron sharpening iron that the Bible talks about has an invaluable, synergistic effect of surrounding yourself with good people who will pull you to a higher level.

Meditate on these scriptures:

> *Poverty and shame shall be to him that refuseth instruction: but he that regardeth reproof shall be honoured.*
>
> Proverbs 13:18

> *If you remain in me and my words remain in you, ask whatever you wish, and it will be given you.*
> *This is to my Father's glory, that you bear much fruit, showing yourselves to be my disciples.*
>
> John 15:7,8 NIV

A good man out of the good treasure of his heart brings forth good; and an evil man out of the evil treasure of his heart brings forth evil. For out of the abundance of the heart his mouth speaks.

Luke 6:45 NKJV

But he who does the truth comes to the light, that his deeds may be clearly seen, that they have been done in God.

John 3:21 NKJV

If I then, your Lord and Teacher, have washed your feet, you also ought to wash one another's feet.

For I have given you an example, that you should do as I have done to you.

Most assuredly, I say to you, a servant is not greater than his master; nor is he who is sent greater than he who sent him.

John 13:14,15 NKJV

Feed the flock of God which is among you, taking the oversight thereof, not by constraint, but willingly; not for filthy lucre, but of a ready mind;

Yea, all of you be subject one to another, and be clothed with humility....

> *Humble yourselves therefore under the mighty hand of God, that he may exalt you in due time.*
>
> 1 Peter 5:2,5,6

Q: What relationships in your life are causing you to increase and grow?

Q: What relationships are causing you to decrease or be stagnant?

Q: What steps do you plan to take to surround yourself with positive, motivating people?

Chapter 12

RECEIVING THE PRIZE

Know ye not that they which run in a race run all, but one receiveth the prize? So run, that ye may obtain.

And every man that striveth for the mastery is temperate in all things. Now they do it to obtain a corruptible crown; but we an incorruptible.

I therefore so run, not as uncertainly; so fight I, not as one that beateth the air:

But I keep under my body, and bring it into subjection: lest that by any means, when I have preached to others, I myself should be a castaway.

1 Corinthians 9:24-27

In 1 Corinthians 9 the apostle Paul said, "Don't you know in a race that all runners run, but only one receives the prize?" And then he encourages us to run so that we might obtain it. He said, "I don't fight like a man beating the air. I make my body my slave. I bring it into subjection so that after I have preached to others, I myself should not be a castaway."

Paul, like Moses, sought the invisible — God — to obtain the imperishable — God's power — so that he could do the impossible — lead a bunch of raggedy Jews up out of captivity. And the apostle Paul said because of Jesus Christ running ahead of us, we are in a fixed race, and we are going to obtain an incorruptible crown.

God wants you to receive the prize — the incorruptible crown — He has for you. It's His reward for diligently seeking Him and being obedient to His call. It isn't an easy race, but here are ten steps to help you maintain until you obtain.

STEP ONE: *Work hard.* When I say work hard, you may think about writing a book, earning a college degree, creating a sales and marketing plan. Others may think in terms of making sales calls, managing a retail store, teaching a class, or building a house. But that's not the work I'm talking about. A number of years ago Charles "Tremendous" Jones taught me that "the real work" is learning to stay excited about your work. Now that takes work!

You may be thinking, *Well, if I was doing what Margie Knight, a talented freelance writer, was doing — working with interesting people and great authors around the country — I could get excited. Or, if I was doing what Joe Knight was doing — great job, getting ready to go into the ministry with prophetic discernment in his life, married to a beautiful woman, a great wife — I could get excited. But if you had my lousy job, you wouldn't talk like that.* The point we make is that all work is lousy! If what you're doing isn't lousy, it probably isn't work.

People don't pay very much money to do the things I like to do. I like to goof off, relax, fellowship, spend time with my wife, go hear other great speakers, read good books. But if I only do what I like to do, at the end of the month when it comes payday, I will find out the things I thought I liked to do, I don't like to do.

E. N. Gray, when he was president of the Prudential Life Insurance Company, wrote an essay called, "The Common Denominator of Success." In this essay, E. N. wrote, "The common denominator of success is simply this. Successful people form the habit of doing things failures don't like to do." You say, "Well, do they like to do it all that much?" The answer is "No!"

I've gone to a meeting and heard some man say, "I love challenge." I feel sorry for the guy. I've always hated challenge. What I like are results. I like results so much that I will put up with some challenge to get results, but I pity the people who love the challenge and get no results. E. N. Gray said that successful people form the habit of doing things failures don't like to do because their focus is on successfully achieving their goals in life. Dr. Hartzell Wilson said, "The things you do that you don't like to do, determine what you are when it's too late to do anything about it."

Successful people form the habit of doing things that failures don't like to do. They do these things religiously. And when it comes payday at the end of the month, they find out that the things they didn't think they liked to do, they DO like to do. There is a price to be paid — different destinations have different prices. Easy jobs don't pay much, and the real work is to get excited about your work even if it isn't something you like to do.

STEP TWO: *Learn to enjoy the climb.* In America today we have the instant success syndrome — the microwave oven, the TV remote control, get these tapes or buy this book and you'll become an overnight, whiz-bang success. We have people adopting self-created credentials and alluding to degrees they haven't really earned. Suzanne Somers says to write and get the "Thigh Master. You'll melt away fifteen ugly pounds in just fifteen minutes a day, three days a week."

That didn't work for my Uncle Bill. He's gotten so big that when he wants a picture taken, we get an aerial photographer. At Christmastime he wears a white sport coat, and we show movies on him. After he stepped on our dog's tail, we had to rename the dog, "Beaver." He's still a big guy.

The point is to enjoy the climb — the process we must go through to receive our prize — and know that in the process, God is developing our character. It is not just obtaining or reaching the goal, but it's learning to enjoy the journey, to enjoy the climb, and to understand if the process is correct and right, then the results at the end will turn out okay.

STEP THREE: *Prepare for tomorrow.* Somebody said these are the last days. If they're not, they're our only days, and the greatest achievements are down the road in our future. The greatest days of ministry in a person's life are just around the corner, and we have to prepare for tomorrow. John Nesbitt said in his book, *Megatrends 2000*, that we are closing in on the final days of possibly the most important decade in the history of civilization.

People are excited about the year 2000, the millennium, the second coming of the Lord Jesus Christ, but Jesus has told us to occupy until He comes. What does that mean? It means getting into the Word, filling our hearts and minds with His wisdom, pursuing education with books, tapes, seminars, and training, learning, and preparing for our future. We're never too old to learn to grow, to develop, to plan, to prepare.

STEP FOUR: *Don't be embarrassed to ask for help.* I explained earlier how I needed to reach out and ask for help in the area of relationships, to receive instruction, to receive ideas on how to grow, how to be a more effective husband, how to do what God has called me to do. Find the resources you need and get help. Men tend to crawl under the covers and hide, to escape. But God said reach out and seek wise counsel. Develop yourself. Talk to people. Do whatever you have to do to build your life.

STEP FIVE: *Find a mentor.* I wouldn't be doing what I am doing today if it had not been for mentorship in my life. I grew up in Grove City, Pennsylvania, a town that was so small, the massage parlor was self-service. We had no heavy industry except for a 300-pound Avon lady. We didn't even have a fire truck, just a big dog that wandered around town when we needed it to put out a fire.

God sent a man to Grove City by the name of Dick Bestwick, who is a living legend today. He has had a long-term, successful career in intercollegiate athletics. He was a great high school football coach, but coming from the difficult home situation I had, he was more than that to me. God used Dick to develop my character, to mentor me, and give me a vision for doing something with my life.

Later God would introduce me to two other fine football coaches by the names of Al Jacks and Chuck Klausing. And then a real life-changing experience for me was to meet and build a friendship and relationship with the great speaker Charles "Tremendous" Jones. Today there are some fine ministers around the country who have mentored me even without their knowing it. For example, to sit in a meeting and watch the teaching and preaching of John Osteen, Rod Parsley, R. W. Schambach, and others has allowed me to draw from their wealth of wisdom of the Word and knowledge of ministry.

Mentorship is important. We don't have to reinvent the wheel. When I was in the insurance business, I would go find agents who were further along in their career and more developed than I was. I asked them if I could simply spend a day with them and watch them to find out what it was they did to be successful and how they did it. Mentorship is incredibly important.

Charles Jones used to store a lot of his books in my garage in Chicago. I would take the books to his meetings, set up the book table, and I thought I was simply being a friend by collecting money and selling some books. Actually, God was using him to show me different speaking techniques, how to work with audiences, and how to set up a room and achieve success by controlling the environment. Mentorship will help a person go to the next level.

STEP SIX: *Be a leader.* You may be thinking, *That leaves me out; I have no leadership potential.* Well, think about this scenario from the Bible. God went to Joshua and said, "I've got some good news and bad news." Joshua, being a positive thinker, said, "What's the bad news?"

God said, "Well, Moses is dead and you're going to be the leader." Joshua said, "You've got the wrong man. Remember, it's me, Joshua. I've never led at anything. My father was a slave and my granddaddy before him was a slave. I came out of a background of 400 years of slavery, and no one in our family has ever led anyone. Now Moses was raised by Pharaoh's daughter, he was a politician, a historian. He was good-looking, like Charleton Heston. And for the frosting on the cake, he took a stick and parted the Red Sea, and you want me to follow him?"

God used Moses because he was available. Like many Christians, when God went to him and said, "I have an assignment for you. I want you to lead My children up out of captivity," Moses tried to get out of it by reminding God he wasn't a public speaker. Moses said, "Lord, You know I can't t-t-t-ta, t-t-t-ta-a-alk real good." God said, "Don't you worry about it, I'll send Aaron to help you. What's that you have in your hand?" Moses said, "It's a r-r-r-rod, Lord." And God said, "Now Moses, you throw that rod down." And of course anyone who has ever been to Sunday school knows that rod became a snake. And God said, "Now Moses, pick that snake up by the tail." And Moses said, "Lord, I can't t-t-t-alk real good and now I don't hear too good either." But God used Moses because he was available.

If you have a choice between someone with great availability and someone with great ability, it is better to take the person with great availability, because many people with great ability are never available. Besides, you don't hire their head, you hire their heart. If their heart is right, their head will line up. If their attitude is right, they can be developed, and you can work with them.

God said to Joshua, "Moses is dead and you're going to be the leader." And Joshua said to God, "The only good news You can give to me is that You're getting ready to raise Moses from the dead." And Joshua had to get up and look at two million raggedy Jews and say, "Hello, I'm your new leader." And these Jews looked at Joshua the same way a raccoon looks at truck headlights and said, "Joshua, what can you do? Can you do the thing with the stick and the water?"

Joshua said, "Please, God, why don't You raise Moses from the dead?" And God said, "No, the good news is that all the things you saw Moses do — he didn't pull it off by himself, I was with him. I moved through him. I empowered him and I was with him. So will I be with you. In fact, Joshua, you won't just go up and look at the Promised Land, you'll possess it and walk in it. You can have everywhere your foot will trod. Get up and get with the program. I'll never leave you. I'll never forsake you. I will empower you, and I will go with you!"

The point to all this is that everyone has leadership ability. Everyone can lead at something, even if it's just at having a good attitude. Dr. Victor Frankel was incarcerated in the Nazi prison camps of World War II. They killed his family and his children, and they burned his manuscripts on logo therapy. But he said, "I can still lead in something. I cannot determine when I'll be beaten, but I can make a decision to have a good attitude. I can't determine when I will be kicked, but I can determine the direction I will go when I have been kicked."

This author of the great book, *Man's Search for Meaning*, began to walk around that prison camp and help keep prisoners alive. He said, "It's Monday. Don't die on Monday, it's a bad day to die." On Tuesday he would say, "Don't die on Tuesday, live until Wednesday." And as he began to keep others alive, he found a purpose for his own life and his own existence. Everybody can make a decision to lead in something. John Maxwell said, "If you think you're a leader and don't have any followers, you are just out for a walk."

STEP SEVEN: *Know your gift. Everybody has a gift.* Somebody said, "Well, this year what I'm doing is making a list of all my weaknesses, and I'm going to perfect my weaknesses." I don't suggest that you do that. When you focus on weakness, all you do is become weaker at what you're already weak at. You say, "If I'm not going to develop my weaknesses, then what should I do?"

Identify your gift or your talent. Know your personality style. Are you a driver, an expressive, an amiable, or an analytical? Know who you are. Know what your gifts are and promote your talent and manage or staff your weakness. Give yourself an opportunity to operate in your gift as many times as possible.

In my book, *Winning 101*, it says this, "Don't ever attempt to teach a pig to sing! It wastes your time and it annoys the pig." The point of that one-liner is, know what you're called to do. Understand your "yes" in life. Know your purpose. What is your destiny? What is your vision?

And then fulfill what you are called to do. You cannot be everything to everybody, and there is no point wasting time wearing yourself out with a multiplicity of goals, visions, and dreams. The apostle Paul said, "This one thing I do." He didn't say these fifteen or twenty things I dabble at. Know your gift and operate in it.

STEP EIGHT: *Set priorities.* A person needs to understand there are only 24 hours in a day, 168 hours in a week, 8,760 hours in a year. The people who get more done are the people who set priorities and make a decision to plan. One hour of planning equals four hours saved. If we don't use our head, then we're going to have to use our feet. We need to understand that someday is not a day of the week. And there is a difference between goals and priorities, as opposed to a New Year's resolution. A person who plans has a greater sense of direction, a greater sense of focus, and a greater sense of protection than all those people who have no focus or direction and want to come and steal your time.

During the 1980s, one of my friends and clients in the insurance business, Walter Payton, was a Hall of Fame member of the National Football League. He was portrayed on the Wheaties box and at Soldiers' Field as sweetness, just a nice young man. He was a nice young man, a nice wealthy young man because of the savings and investments he had made.

But Walter was also one of the most competitive men I have ever met in my life. I asked him one day, "In the National Football League, when the average man plays less than four years, how have you lasted thirteen?" He said, "The Chicago Bears suggested that I train at one level, but I made a decision to train at the next highest level. I didn't let big men who were big enough to eat hay and dumb enough to enjoy it careen into my body — you know, those 300-pounders. I made them pay a price to bring me down. And as my record began to unfold, I made a decision to run up records that the average person would have a difficult time ever breaking. I made a decision to be the best that I could become."

We've got to develop a set of priorities. Nike says we've got to "Just do it."

STEP NINE: *Forget your past mistakes*. Here's a great line from my friend, Mike Murdock: "God never consults your past to determine your future." There is no future in your past. The apostle Paul said,

> *I do not count myself to have apprehended; but one thing I do, forgetting those things which are behind and reaching forward to those things which are ahead, I press toward the goal for the prize of the upward call of God in Christ Jesus.*
>
> Philippians 3:13,14 NKJV

What was his high calling? Philippians 3:10 NKJV says,

> *That I may know Him and the power of His resurrection, and the fellowship of His sufferings, being conformed to His death.*

The word "resurrection" is an interesting word in the Greek. One of the few times it is used in the New Testament, it has the prefix in English before it and means, "the exit, the out-resurrection, how to come alive among the walking dead."[1]

You cannot unscramble eggs, but God can take those scrambled eggs and turn them into a very nice soufflé. There is no point in looking back unless that is the direction we plan to go, and we don't plan to go that way.

STEP TEN: *Don't quit.* Anytime you make a decision to go to the next level there is always going to come a time when you feel like quitting. It's normal and natural. It's not anti-spiritual. Because of the pressures and calamities of life, the challenges of life, there's always going to be a time when a person wants to quit. But just because you want to quit doesn't mean you have to quit.

Today in my life I can enjoy the occasional feeling of wanting to quit because I know I'm not going to quit. That thought has got a different perspective, and when we think that we have come to the end, many times we are just at the beginning. Stay, fight, stand, and go on.

When you've come to the end of your rope, tie a knot and hang on. When the devil finds out he cannot run you off, you won't give in, you won't fade in the face of adversity, then he will move on to someone else when he sees that you refuse to move. So, don't quit! Claim your prize. It's yours. Jesus already paid for it. It's up to you to reach out and receive it.

Meditate on these scriptures:

> *Where there is no vision, the people perish: but*
> *he that keepeth the law, happy is he.*
>
> *Proverbs 29:18*

But he who trusts in me shall possess the land and inherit my Holy Mountain.

The high and lofty one who inhabits eternity, the Holy One, says this: I live in that high and holy place where those with contrite, humble spirits dwell; and I refresh the humble and give new courage to those with repentant hearts.

Isaiah 57:13,15 TLB

As for me, this is my covenant with them, saith the Lord; My spirit that is upon thee, and my words which I have put in thy mouth, shall not depart out of thy mouth, nor out of the mouth of thy seed, nor out of the mouth of thy seed's seed, saith the Lord, from henceforth and for ever.

Isaiah 59:21

O Lord, thou art our father; we are the clay, and thou our potter; and we all are the work of thy hand.

Isaiah 64:8

And shall put my spirit in you, and ye shall live, and I shall place you in your own land: then shall ye know that I the Lord have spoken it, and performed it, saith the Lord.

Ezekiel 37:14

For by thy words thou shalt be justified, and by thy words thou shalt be condemned.

Matthew 12:37

And Jesus said unto them, Verily I say unto you, That ye which have followed me, in the regeneration when the Son of man shall sit in the throne of his glory, ye also shall sit upon twelve thrones, judging the twelve tribes of Israel.

And every one that hath forsaken houses, or brethren, or sisters, or father, or mother, or wife, or children, or lands, for my name's sake, shall receive an hundredfold, and shall inherit everlasting life.

Matthew 19:28,29

Verily, verily, I say unto you, If a man keep my saying, he shall never see death.

John 8:51

My sheep hear my voice, and I know them, and they follow me:

And I give unto them eternal life; and they shall never perish, neither shall any man pluck them out of my hand.

John 10:27,28

I am the resurrection, and the life: he that believeth in me, though he were dead, yet shall he live.

John 11:25

Verily, verily, I say unto you, He that believeth on me, the works that I do shall he do also; and greater works than these shall he do; because I go unto my Father.

John 14:12

In my Father's house are many mansions: if it were not so, I would have told you. I go to prepare a place for you.

John 14:2

Whatsoever ye shall ask the Father in my name, he will give it you.

Hitherto have ye asked nothing in my name: ask, and ye shall receive, that your joy may be full.

John 16:23,24

If ye then be risen with Christ, seek those things which are above, where Christ sitteth on the right hand of God.

Set your affection on things above, not on things on the earth.

For ye are dead, and your life is hid with Christ in God.

When Christ, who is our life, shall appear, then shall ye also appear with him in glory.

Colossians 3:1-4

"For I know the plans I have for you," declares the Lord, "plans to prosper you and not to harm you, plans to give you hope and a future.

"Then you will call upon me and come and pray to me, and I will listen to you.

"You will seek me and find me when you seek me with all your heart."

Jeremiah 29:11-13 NIV

Q: Do you see your calling as a prize, a treasure? Why or why not?

Q: Where do you place your priorities and confidence regarding your calling?

Q: What memories and hurts from the past will you put behind you today?

Q: What action will you take to discover the incredible future God has for you?

Conclusion

MORE THAN A CONQUEROR

*Yet in all these things we are more than
conquerors through Him who loved us.*

*For I am persuaded that neither death nor life,
nor angels nor principalities nor powers, nor things
present nor things to come,*

*Nor height nor depth, nor any other created
thing, shall be able to separate us from the love of
God which is in Christ Jesus our Lord.*

Romans 8:37-39 NKJV

In November 1996 I had a spiritual experience. You
say, "Was it in a church?" No, it was in a bowling alley
outside of Toledo late one Saturday night. Although I was
going to be preaching early the next morning, a friend
insisted we go watch a boxer by the name of Evander
Holyfield — who happened to be a Christian — go into
the ring against an avowed Muslim.

We drove out to the bowling alley to watch Evander
Holyfield go into the ring against Mike Tyson. (They
weren't actually fighting in the bowling alley. We were
just watching it on the television at the bowling alley.)
The sports prognosticators had given Holyfield no hope
and did not expect the fight to last more than three

rounds. Some places were selling the fight to their customers on a "pay-per-round" basis, thinking the fight would not last more than nine minutes. Evander Holyfield was a 25-to-1 underdog.

If you watched that fight, you saw Evander Holyfield stand in his corner and pray between rounds. In round six he hit Tyson in the chest with a hard right and sent him to the canvas. In round eleven the fight was stopped and Holyfield was declared the winner. Evander Holyfield had beaten him from head to toe, and it's a wonder the police didn't come in and arrest Mike Tyson for impersonating a piñata.

After this incredible upset, Evander Holyfield sat at the press conference on national television, wearing a baseball cap which said, "Jesus is Lord!" and a tee shirt which said, "Blood Bought." I sat there, thrilled that he was giving a clear-cut testimony for our Lord Jesus Christ. He came across as a man of character, honor, and integrity.

In 1997 God took me to an even higher level in the second Holyfield-Tyson fight. The stakes were high — a $35 million purse — as Mike Tyson entered the ring looking like Mr. T. in the movie, *Rocky III*. In round three the most amazing thing happened. Tyson, understanding he was already in trouble, proceeded to bite the ears of Evander Holyfield! The fight was stopped, Tyson was disqualified, and Evander Holyfield was named the winner — yes, even a conqueror. It took Evander nine minutes of aerobics to win $35 million.

When Evander Holyfield walked into his house that night, he had a welt on his head and big holes in each ear. He sat down in his favorite recliner to rest and relax, and Mrs. Holyfield walked around the corner and said, "How much did WE win?" Evander's a conqueror, but you know what Mrs. Holyfield is? Mrs. Holyfield is *more than a conqueror*. She didn't do any of the fighting, but she intends to participate in that $35 million purse!

Now don't start thinking Mrs. Holyfield is greedy, because she is a picture of exactly what we are in Jesus Christ — more than conquerors. Jesus did the fighting and won the victory, just like Evander Holyfield did, and we get to participate in the victory as *more* than conquerors, just like Mrs. Holyfield did. She expected to participate, and so should we!

Jesus did the dying so we could do the living. Jesus took our sicknesses upon Himself so we could be well. Jesus became poor so we could be rich. You and I have been made more than conquerors through our Lord Jesus Christ. It would have been wonderful if the Bible would have said we were just conquerors, but no, the Bible makes it clear that we have been made *more* than conquerors.

Are you ready to possess your land? This is your time to be *more* than a conqueror — to participate in the joy of living and receive the riches Jesus won for you on the cross. You now have all the tools you need to cross the Jordan and take back what is rightfully yours.

If you followed the steps in this book as you read along, you've already 1) faced your hour of decision, 2) determined in your heart not to blame God for your circumstances now or in the future, 3) humbled yourself before the Lord and repented of your sins to God and to others as needed, 4) purposed to do what's right to make amends and restitution, 5) developed a new focus by getting your eyes off the circumstances and onto the solution, 6) learned how to resist the devil to make him flee, 7) developed a praise mentality, 8) dressed yourself in battle armor, sharpened your weapons, and developed a proactive strategy for waging war on the devil, 9) explored ways to discern God-given relationships, 10) committed to putting first things first in your relationships, 11) scrutinized the value of accountability, and 12) discovered the incredible future God has for you.

Did you realize you had done all that? It's a lot to digest all at once, but you are an overcomer! You've got what it takes. You may not be an expert marksman yet, but as you apply the tried and tested principles you have learned, you will gain ground, one hilltop at a time.

You didn't get where you are overnight, and you won't be where you want to be by tomorrow. So stop beating yourself up at every setback and start patting yourself on the back for every bit of territory you've taken. Wars are won battle by battle and skirmish by skirmish.

When Joshua and the Israelites crossed the Jordan, they had to take back the land one battle at a time. But the Lord was with them, and when they were obedient to do what He told them to do, He went before them and they were victorious. God was faithful to fulfill the word He had given to Joshua, and Joshua TRUSTED his God.

Trust is a big word, but it is the key to your future. The word "trust" is found in the Bible (KJV) 134 times — 107 times in the Old Testament and 27 times in the New Testament. At least 40 percent of those verses speak of the benefits or rewards we receive for trusting in our God.

Will you trust Him?

Here's what you will receive: The inheritance of your promised land, everlasting strength, safety, the heritage of those who fear His name, refuge, salvation, glory, joy, help, deliverance, love, prosperity and true riches, lovingkindness, hope, an absence of confusion, a shield of protection, redemption, a drink of living water. These are just some of the blessings and benefits.

Will you believe in all He has promised and claim it as your own?

How much are such blessings and benefits worth to you?

Here's what David told the Lord after he had been rescued from Saul.

> The Lord is my rock, and my fortress, and my deliverer;
>
> The God of my rock; in him will I trust: he is my shield, and the horn of my salvation, my high tower, and my refuge, my saviour; thou savest me from violence.
>
> I will call on the Lord, who is worthy to be praised: so shall I be saved from mine enemies.
>
> In my distress I called upon the Lord, and cried to my God: and he did hear my voice out of his temple, and my cry did enter into his ears.
>
> 2 Samuel 22:2-4,7

A great price is always attached to something of great value. Things that come too easy or at no cost have little value and often are not appreciated. Are you willing to pay the price to obtain such benefits? David was rewarded for his righteousness, but he had to pay the price of obedience.

> The Lord rewarded me according to my righteousness: according to the cleanness of my hands hath he recompensed me.
>
> For I have kept the ways of the Lord, and have not wickedly departed from my God.

For all his judgments were before me: and as for his statues, I did not depart from them.

I was also upright before him, and have kept myself from iniquity.

Therefore the Lord hath recompensed me according to my righteousness; according to my cleanness in his eye sight.

As for God, his way is perfect; the word of the Lord is tried: he is a buckler to all them that trust in him.

2 Samuel 22:21-25,31

You're at a critical jumping off point right now. Imagine yourself standing in the door of an airplane with a parachute strapped on your back. You've never sky-dived before, and the pilot just announced the plane's engine is on fire. The choice is clear. You either jump and trust the parachute to take you safely to earth, or you crash and die. In real life, you must either trust in the love and promises of your God and live, or trust the devil and his lies and die. It's just that black and white.

If you don't believe God, then who do you believe? The only other alternative is to believe some human being who's probably no smarter than you or the devil. You can't trust in the words of other men or in the earthly possessions of this world. There is no middle ground. It's life or death!

This is your hour of decision! I challenge you to choose life, that you and your family may live. Walk in the integrity of God's Word and the reality of His redemption, and the greatest days of your life, relationships, and career are just around the corner!

I would encourage you to meditate on these scriptures and note the highlighted portions that emphasize the benefits of trusting in the living God:

> *But he that putteth his trust in me shall **possess the land**, and shall **inherit my holy mountain**.*
>
> Isaiah 57:13

> *The Lord thy God in the midst of thee is mighty; he will **save**, he will **rejoice over thee with joy**; he will rest in his love, **he will joy over thee with singing**.*
>
> Zephaniah 3:17

> *And they were helped against them, and the Hagrites were **delivered into their hand**, and all who were with them, for they cried out to God in the battle. **He heeded their prayer**, because they put their trust in Him.*
>
> 1 Chronicles 5:20 NKJV

But let all those that put their trust in thee rejoice: let them ever shout for joy, because thou defendest them: let them also that love thy name be joyful in thee.

For thou, Lord, wilt bless the righteous; with favour wilt thou compass him as with a shield.

Psalm 5:11,12

And they that know thy name will put their trust in thee: for thou, Lord, hast not forsaken them that seek thee.

Psalm 9:10

Trust in the Lord, and do good; so shalt thou dwell in the land, and verily thou shalt be fed.

Delight thyself also in the Lord; and he shall give thee the desires of thine heart.

Psalm 37:3,4

How precious is your constant love, O God! All humanity takes refuge in the shadow of your wings.

You feed them with blessings from your own table and let them drink from your rivers of delight.

Psalm 36:7,8 TLB

And he hath put a new song in my mouth, even praise unto our God: **many shall see it, and fear, and shall trust in the Lord.**

Psalm 40:3

Cast thy burdens upon the Lord, and he shall sustain thee: he shall never suffer the righteous to be moved.

But thou, O God, shalt bring them down into the pit of destruction: bloody and deceitful men shall not live out half their days; but I will trust in thee.

Psalm 55:22,23

Be merciful unto me, O God, be merciful unto me: for my soul trusteth in thee: yea, **in the shadow of thy wings will I make my refuge, until these calamities be overpast.**

Psalm 57:1

In God have I put my trust: **I will not be afraid what man can do unto me.**

Psalm 56:11

I will abide in thy tabernacle for ever: I will trust in the covert of thy wings. Selah.

For thou, O God, hast heard my vows: thou hast **given me the heritage of those that fear thy name.**

Psalm 61:4,5

Charge them that are rich in this world, that they be not highminded, nor trust in uncertain riches, but in the living God, who **giveth us richly all things to enjoy.**

1 Timothy 6:17

A greedy man stirs up dissension, but **he who trusts in the Lord will prosper.**

Proverbs 28:25 NIV

The Lord is good, **a strong hold in the day of trouble**; *and he knoweth them that trust in him.*

Nahum 1:7

Cause me to **hear thy lovingkindness** *in the morning; for in thee do I trust: cause me to* **know the way wherein I should walk**; *for I lift up my soul unto thee.*

Psalm 143:8

ENDNOTES

Chapter 1

[1] Kenneth Blanchard and Spencer Johnson, *The One Minute Manager*. (New York, New York: Berkley Books, 1982), 19.

Chapter 2

George Barna, *What Americans Believe* (Ventura, California: Regal Books, 1991), 204-206.

Chapter 3

James Robison, *Blockages to Communication* (Fort Worth, Texas: James Robison Evangelistic Association, 1982), 6.

[2] Creflo A. Dollar, *Hearing from God and Walking in the Comfort of the Holy Spirit* (College Park, Georgia: Creflo A. Dollar Jr., 1994), 6.

Chapter 4

[1] Robison, *Blockages to Communication*, 4.

[2] *Institute in Basic Youth Conflicts: Research in Principles of Life* (United States: Institute in Basic Youth Conflicts, 1979), 50-55.

[3] Ibid.

Chapter 5

[1] Terry Moore, "Spiritual Warfare" (Sermon on Audiocassette) Carrollton, Texas: Sojourn Church, March 16, 1997.

[2] Ibid.

Chapter 6

[1] Kenneth E. Hagin, *The Believer's Authority* (Tulsa, Oklahoma: Rhema Bible Church, 1984), 24.

Chapter 7

[1] Merlin Carothers, *Prison to Praise* (Escondido, California: Foundation of Praise, 1970), 98-99.

Chapter 8

[1] Kenneth Hagin, Jr., *Faith Takes Back What the Devil's Stolen* (Tulsa, Oklahoma: Rhema Bible Church, 1982), 4-5.

[2] *Webster's Ninth New Collegiate Dictionary*, s.v. "wrestle."

[3] Ibid, s.v. "take."

[4] *Biblesoft's New Exhaustive Strong's Number and Concordance with Expanded Greek-Hebrew Dictionary*, s.v. "take."

[5] *Matthew Henry's Commentary on the Whole Bible: New Modern Edition* (Peabody, Massachusetts: Hendrickson Publishers Inc., 1991), Matt. 11:13.

[6] Brock and Bodie Thoene, *The Twilight of Courage* (Nashville: Thomas Nelson Publishers, 1994), 453.

[7] *Webster's Ninth New Collegiate Dictionary*, s.v. "destroy."

[8] Stephen R. Covey, *The 7 Habits of Highly Effective People* (New York, New York: Simon & Schuster, 1989), 65.

[9] Charles E. Jones, *Eternal Life Insurance Company* (Camp Hill, Pennsylvania: Life Management Services Inc.).

Chapter 12

[1] *Vine's Complete Expository Dictionary of Old and New Testament Words*, s.v. "resurrection."

ABOUT THE AUTHOR

Van Crouch is widely known as one of the most entertaining and thought-provoking speakers in America. As the founder and president of the consulting firm, Van Crouch Communications, he presents a powerful challenge to individuals to achieve excellence in their lives.

After being a sales leader with the American Express Company, Van went on to receive many awards for outstanding performance in the insurance industry, including qualifying as a member of the Million Dollar Round Table.

Van authored the bestselling book, *Stay in the Game*.

Van is in demand to do seminars and as a keynote speaker to Fortune 500 companies, government organizations, church groups, and management and sales conventions worldwide.

Van Crouch has the ability to motivate people to raise their level of expectation. He is sure to both inspire and challenge you.

To contact Van Crouch write:

Van Crouch Communications
P. O. Box 320
Wheaton, Illinois 60187

Additional copies of this book and other
book titles from ALBURY PUBLISHING
are available at your local bookstore.

ALBURY PUBLISHING
P. O. Box 470406
Tulsa, Oklahoma 74147-0406

In Canada books are available from:
Word Alive
P. O. Box 670
Niverville, Manitoba
CANADA ROA 1EO